Family Celebrations

Family Celebrations

Meeting Christ in Your Holidays and Special Occasions

Ann Hibbard

Wolgemuth & Hyatt, Publishers, Inc.
Brentwood, Tennessee

Unless otherwise noted, all Scripture quotations are from
the Holy Bible, New International Version. Copyright 1973,
1978, 1984 International Bible Society. Used by permission of
Zondervan Bible Publishers.

Wolgemuth & Hyatt, Publishers, Inc.
P.O. Box 1941, Brentwood, Tennessee 37027.

Printed in the United States of America.

Library of Congress Cataloging-in-Publication Data

Hibbard, Ann, 1956-
    Family celebrations : meeting Christ in your holidays and
    special occasions — 1st ed.
    p.   cm.
ISBN 0-943497-36-1
    1. Christian education—Home training.
    2. Family—Religious life.
    3. Holidays—United States.
    4. Church year.   I. Title.

BV1590.H48   1988   249—dc19   88-27468

To my husband, Jim,
and our children, Mark and Laura

CONTENTS

ACKNOWLEDGMENTS

The hands of many Christian parents and children alike helped to shape this book. The families of Falls Church Episcopal, particularly the dear friends in our Family Life Action Group, tried out many of these ideas. Their enthusiasm, support, and suggestions have proven invaluable to me.

Without the prayers and encouragement of those closest to me, this book would still be merely a dream. Debbie Bennetch, Linda Garnier, Susan Yates, and Beth Spring have prayed for me and cheered me on during the past five months of writing. I am especially thankful for my husband Jim's infinite patience and unflagging support. Sweetest of all were the prayers of our children, Laura and Mark.

I am deeply grateful to my publishers, Michael Hyatt and Robert Wolgemuth, for believing in me. My editor, George Grant, assisted me in countless ways throughout the project. I would also like to thank Tom Minnery, my editor at Focus on the Family, for nurturing my writing career.

Role models played a significant part in the development of our family celebrations. Bonnie Addington, Skip Sellers, and Susan Yates, three extraordinarily creative Christian parents, inspired and challenged me. A special thanks goes to Tim Addington, who scrutinized my manuscript for theological orthodoxy.

Finally, I am indebted to those who laid the spiritual foundation in my life, my parents, Marilynn Martin and Lester Martin, and my two sisters, Elaine Nesbit and Carolyn Martin, as well as the family of Minnetonka Community Church.

WHY CELEBRATE?

Twenty kindergarteners stood in one, long, disheveled row, bedecked in Pilgrim hats and Indian headdresses made from colorful construction paper. Their parents sat awkwardly in tiny chairs at tiny tables, eyes glued to their own little cherubs. An aura of joyful festivity filled the room. With some prompting from the teachers, the children proudly sang their song about turkeys, complete with hand motions.

It was Miss Martin's annual Thanksgiving feast. The children were the Pilgrim and Indian hosts and served their parents a delicious Thanksgiving meal (dishes prepared and brought by the parents, of course). Having been through this procedure last year with my son Mark, I was an old hand and thus qualified as a server.

As I scooped sweet potatoes and pierced slices of turkey, I chatted with the mother of one of Laura's classmates. Wendy was a single parent, friendly and outgoing, eager to share the joys and concerns of her personal life. She told me of the wonderful man in her life who loved her son Tommy as his own. In fact, he planned to legally adopt him when they married the following May. Our conversation turned to the upcoming Christmas season.

"I always wanted a family Christmas that was more than just presents," she confided. "When I was growing up, my family always held hands around the Christmas tree and sang Christmas carols.

"I never told Rick about that," she continued. "But do you know what he said the other day? He said, 'Wendy, I want our Christmas to be special, a real family Christmas. Before we open presents, let's stand around the Christmas tree, holding hands, and sing a Christmas carol.' I knew then that we were meant to be a family."

Soon the plates were all filled and the children sat beside their parents at the miniature tables, poised to dive into the food. There was a brief, uncomfortable silence.

"Children, it's Thanksgiving! What do we say to the parents who brought these good things?" prompted the teacher.

"Thank you!" the children cried in unison. Everyone commenced eating, the tension lifted.

How sad, I thought to myself. It would have been most appropriate to say a prayer. After all, that is what Thanksgiving is all about—thanking God for his care for us. But our culture has shut God out of Thanksgiving as it has the rest of "public life."

Yet people still crave the security and joy that come from the timeless family traditions, rooted in Biblical Christianity. Like Wendy, they long for something deeper than a "Hallmark card holiday."

Reclaiming Our Territory

Christian families hold the key to joyful, exciting family celebrations. Knowing Christ infuses all of life with joy and meaning—especially holidays and special occasions. At the heart of these special times are events that focus on Christ's life and the teaching of the Scriptures. Christmas and Easter are Christian holy days celebrating Jesus' birth, death for our sins, and glorious resurrection. Valentine's Day, Thanksgiving, and All Saints' Day (as opposed to Halloween) find their source in Christian tradition and are meant to celebrate Christian themes.

The significance of these holidays is all but lost in our secularized society. Baby Jesus has been usurped by a secular Santa, the risen Lord has been pushed aside by the Easter bunny, and Thanksgiving is explained as a celebration of friendship with the Indians.

Christians need to reclaim the territory of our spiritual heritage. The onus lies on us, as Christian parents, to entrust our children with the true significance of these special occasions. Our celebrations must be distinctive, for the sake of our children and of a Christ-less world. If Christ is the center of our lives and our homes, naturally our holidays and special occasions should reflect this priority.

When we do seek to put Christ in the center of our family celebrations, however, we struggle to get beyond the superficial trappings thrust upon us by our culture. Santa and the Easter bunny loom larger than life. How can we break through the "visions of sugar plums" that dance in our children's heads to communicate the spiritual significance of these holidays and special times — without quenching our children's excitement?

The Joy of Anticipation

Perhaps we can take a lesson from the early church. Right from the beginning those faithful Christians introduced the practice of "spiritual preparation" for holy days (from which comes our word *holidays*). Christmas and Easter were preceded by periods of disciplined anticipation (study, contemplation, repentance, prayer, and fasting), so that believers would be spiritually ready to celebrate Christ's birth or resurrection. This also served to extend the celebration from a one-day event to an entire season.

This idea is perfectly suited to children, for they have a natural gift of anticipation. They seem virtually to live for holidays and special occasions. No sooner do they finish celebrating one such occasion than they begin eagerly planning for the next festive event. Children even measure time by holidays and special occasions. "How many days until Christmas?" "Is that before or after my birthday?" These are the high points of the year; ordinary days pale in comparison.

This book is a guide for family celebrations that builds on children's love of holidays and their joy of anticipation. For each holiday and special occasion, a specific plan is laid out for the family to prepare for that event. A family project or holiday craft doubles as a teaching tool during the days or weeks leading up to the occasion. Family times around God's Word during this season focus the family's attention on the spiritual principles which underlie that holiday. Each chapter concludes with a plan for making the actual holiday celebration special. Some celebrations consist of a service of family worship, some include instructions for a fun family game, activity, or party. All are guaranteed to kindle the imagination and spark ideas for exciting, meaningful family celebrations.

By extending the joyful celebration of special occasions over a longer period, Christian parents have the time and opportunity to underscore the special significance of these holidays. For instance, all the teaching about Jesus' resurrection does not have to be crammed into the same twenty-four hours that you are hunting for Easter eggs, dressing up for church, and preparing a meal. The family will have been examining for the previous eight weeks the significance of Jesus' death and resurrection. The specialness of those family times instills in children a sense of the importance of their religious heritage. Preparing for Easter in this way, we give Jesus preeminence.

Perhaps most important, Christian family celebrations need to be fun. If "spiritual" becomes synonymous with "boring," the battle is already lost. Children don't come into the world with that association—it is learned. They are just as ready to believe that the Bible is an exciting book filled with true adventure stories. Family times spent focusing on Jesus and truth can be amusing and entertaining as well as serious. Laughter is a wonderful gift that can bind us together, lighten our hearts, and give us perspective.

If our family times are full to the brim with laughter and encouragement, our children will soak up truth like sponges. Those family times will become very important to them, and they will look forward to next year's repeat performance with enthusiasm. Spiritual preparation will become an essential ingredient in the family's holiday traditions.

Lifetime Memories

Family celebrations create memories that last a lifetime. Most of us hold fond recollections of special birthdays and things our family did every Christmas. These images are precious to us. As children arrive on the scene, we possess a deep desire for our children to experience the traditions that made our own childhood so special.

My conversation with Wendy during the Thanksgiving feast revealed Wendy's longing for joy and meaning in their family celebrations. For Christian parents, however, holding hands and singing a Christmas carol may not be sufficient if we want the Lord to permeate every facet of our special occasions.

The question is, how? Perhaps we don't feel creative enough to come up with our own Christ-centered traditions. Furthermore, it sounds like too much work. If only there were a book with a step-by-step plan for celebrating each holiday and special occasion in a fun, exciting, and Christ-centered way. *Family Celebrations* is that book.

HOW TO USE THIS BOOK

Family Celebrations is geared to families with elementary school-aged children. Activities and discussion questions can easily be modified to suit younger and older children as well. Feel free to adapt these ventures to the age levels of your children.

The introduction to each chapter indicates when the time of preparation for that holiday begins. If you pick up the book only to discover that you have missed the first three weeks of the Christmas family times, don't be dismayed. Just begin where you are, at the final week. Next year you can start your celebration earlier.

Each chapter presents a complete plan for the spiritual celebration of a holiday or special occasion. Here are the basic elements that you'll find:

INTRODUCTION

Opening with a brief story, the introduction to each chapter provides some basic background information on the celebration of that holiday, as well as an overview of the chapter.

FAMILY PROJECT

The family project ideally should be undertaken at the beginning of the time of preparation. Most of the projects can be used during the subsequent family times as visual aids and teaching tools to reinforce Scriptural truth. However, they are not absolutely necessary to the celebration. Suggested projects can be changed, improved on, or deleted, according to each family's talents or preferences. Once completed, however, most of the proposed projects last virtually for a lifetime and may be reused year after year in celebrating that holiday.

FAMILY TIMES AROUND GOD'S WORD

Family times around God's Word really comprise the heart of *Family Celebrations*. They offer a thoroughgoing format for creative family learning from the Scriptures. These family times take place during the weeks preceding the holiday. In most cases, there is one family time per week.

Each family time includes:

1. A Bible story or brief passage. For younger children, don't read it; merely tell it in your own words.

2. Discussion questions, simple but thought-provoking. Modify these to suit the age level of your children if necessary.

3. Something to do. There is a simple assignment to help apply the Scripture to everyday life.

4. Bible memory verse. Many of these verses are put to music in the "God's Word for Today's Kids" tapes, a musical Scripture memory series featuring G. T. and the Halo Express.

5. A brief family prayer. Don't feel limited to the suggested prayer. Encourage your children to pray extemporaneously as well. They may have something on their minds they would like to bring to God.

6. A hymn. Only the words are given to an old hymn of the faith. Sing if you know the tune; otherwise, simply read the words. Or substitute an appropriate favorite. Or skip it altogether if little ones are getting antsy.

A good hymnal is a great aid in family worship. There are many such hymnals on the market today, readily available in Christian bookstores and surprisingly inexpensive. All of the hymns in this book can be found in the *Hymnal for Worship and Celebration*, published by Word Music, 1986, Waco, TX. Along with the hymn names, I have given the hymn number in this particular hymnal. For instance, "Amazing Grace" (*HWC* 202) means that you can find the music and complete text for that hymn in the *Hymnal for Worship and Celebration*, and it is hymn number 202.

FAMILY CELEBRATION

Each chapter concludes with instructions for making the actual holiday celebration special. Modify and improve upon these suggestions to suit the unique character of your family.

Be flexible, and have fun!

Welcome, all wonders in one sight!
   Eternity shut in a span,
Summer in winter, day in night,
   Heaven in earth, and God in man!
Great little One, whose all-embracing birth
Lifts earth to Heaven, stoops Heav'n to earth.

Richard Crashaw, 1612-1649
"In the Holy Nativity of Our Lord God"

COME LET US ADORE HIM

Christmas

The worshipers huddled together against the cold of the December night. Before them a gnarled oak tree stood black against a star-swept sky. A small boy lay stretched on an altar at the base of the tree. Over him loomed a hideous figure — the High Priest of Thor. The crowd stood mesmerized as the High Priest slowly raised a huge hammer high over his head.

Just as the hammer began to descend toward the boy, a black-robed man thrust himself through the crowd. He stretched forth a Cross which caught the blow of the hammer.

The worshipers gasped. Stupefied with fear, the High Priest let the hammer fall to the ground and backed away. Surely at any moment, Thor would strike down this intruder.

But there was no angry recourse from the heavens. The black-robed man, Boniface, released the boy.

"Tonight this oak shall be felled!" Boniface declared. With phenomenal energy, he delivered blow after blow to the ancient tree. Finally, it crashed to the ground.

Turning to the silent crowd, Boniface told them of the true God who loved them and sent His own Son to give them life. No more must they perform such rites of death.

His eye caught a young pine tree, its green boughs stretched toward heaven.

"Here is the living tree," he said. "Bring this tree into the light of your homes to remind you of the everlasting life that is yours in Christ. This tree shall be called the tree of the Christ-child, for tonight we celebrate the birth of the Savior."

INTRODUCTION

Background

This is the story of the first Christmas tree. It reminds us of the everlasting life that Christ came to bring sinners and the sacrificial courage that marked the efforts of early missionaries like Boniface to tell the world of that glorious Good News. The Christmas season is rich with Christian reminders. But, as in the case of the Christmas tree, these symbols have become so secularized that in many cases their meaning has been lost or forgotten.

The candy cane, for instance, is meant to represent the shepherd's crook. Its white body stands for holiness, the red stripes for Christ's blood shed on our account. Even the flavor of peppermint recalls the Biblical herb hyssop, which was used as flavoring and as medicine. That points to Christ's ministry of healing and the wholeness he made available to all.

The modern Santa Claus finds his origin in a young pastor named Nicholas. His parents died when he was still a boy, leaving him a fortune. He loved the Lord and cared deeply for those in need. Not wanting to receive any glory himself, he went secretly, during the night, to the homes of poor families. There he left gifts and money because of his love for Christ.

This chapter focuses on the Christian distinctives of the Christmas season. Traditionally, the church celebration of Christmas begins with Advent (four Sundays before Christmas), and concludes with Epiphany (January 6). Extending the season in this way allows us to explore all the spiritual principles that come to bear upon this wonderful event.

Advent means *coming*. Advent is a time to prepare our hearts both for Christ's second coming and for celebrating His first coming.

The observance of Advent greatly enriches the Christmas season. By setting aside a few moments each day to meditate on Christ—the mystery of the Incarnation and the reason for His coming—our hearts are made in tune with His. As we read the prophesies that foretell Christ's coming, we catch the spirit of eager anticipation. Gabriel's visit to Mary instills in us a sense of mystery and beauty. Then we turn the pages to Joseph and Mary's trek to Bethlehem. For the Christian celebrating Advent, Christmas is the climactic conclusion to an incredible story.

The mood of Advent is a blend of joy and solemnity. Spiritual preparation involves sorrow for sin — after all, Jesus came to die for our sins. (The color purple is used to symbolize repentance and is used in Advent candles and linens.) But the sorrow is a good sorrow, which lasts only for a time, to be followed by the joy of forgiveness. Happy excitement builds as the celebration of His birth draws near.

Children can teach us much about joyful anticipation. Christmas is on their minds every day of December (probably November as well). As the day approaches, their excitement builds to a fever pitch. If they didn't think about it so much beforehand, they would not experience such ecstasy. Likewise, the spiritual preparation of Advent enables us to experience more fully the excitement of His coming. Christmas becomes a more joyful and more sacred event in the life of the family.

Epiphany means *manifestation*. It especially celebrates the visit of the Magi to Jesus, whose birth was manifested by a star. In a larger sense, Epiphany proclaims that God was manifested to the world in the person of His Son, Jesus Christ.

In earlier times, this was an important day — a festival observed by attending church services and pageants, exchanging gifts, and feasting with family and friends.

A modern-day celebration of Epiphany offers many advantages. The party can be planned and enjoyed in the relaxation of the post-Christmas season. It allows one final opportunity to sing all the favorite Christmas carols and recall all the beautiful Scriptures of Advent. Most important, it reiterates the significance of Christ's coming in a way which is memorable to our children.

Overview

The twenty-four family times during Advent prepare our hearts to celebrate His birth on Christmas. These times of family worship center around the Scriptures, using as visual aids an Advent tree with a corresponding symbol to add daily and a traditional Advent wreath.

The first three family times (December 1-3) might be entitled "Jesus: Eternal with the Father." The passages show that Jesus existed before He was born in Bethlehem, even before the creation of the world.

"Jesus: Sent to Save Sinners" is the second focus of our family times (December 4-8). These family times look at why Jesus came to earth.

The family times for December 9-17 reveal Jesus as the fulfillment of Old Testament prophecy. In "Jesus: Spoken of by the Prophets," we will read prophecies that foretell His purpose (9-11), His character (12-14), and His coming (15-17).

Lastly, during the final week of Advent (December 18-24) we will turn to the pages of Matthew and Luke which record the events surrounding the Lord's birth—"Jesus: Born of the Virgin Mary."

A format for family worship on Christmas is included. This may be used on Christmas Eve or Christmas Day, according to your family tradition.

A fun, new tradition is a Twelfth Night Party on January 6 (the twelfth night after Christmas). This should provide an exciting and reinforcing conclusion to your family's celebration of Christ's birth.

FAMILY PROJECT

Two family projects are included in this section. Both are designed to enhance and reinforce the family times during Advent (December 1-24), as your family learns about Christ's coming and prepares to celebrate His birth.

The first project is an Advent Tree Banner. Each day of Advent, a symbol is added to the tree as a part of your family time around the Word. The symbol corresponds to the Scripture reading for that day. Instructions are given for making a felt banner with felt symbols. This banner will last for years to come. For a simpler, less permanent alternative, see Other Ideas, #4, page 14.

The second project is an Advent Wreath. This can be purchased or home-made. Several suggestions are offered for making your own wreath. It can be as simple or as elaborate as you choose to make it. The Advent Wreath reminds us of the light of Jesus Christ coming into the world. The lighting of the candles creates a worshipful mood for the family times during this sacred season.

Advent Tree Banner

Materials

- ⅝ yard of 36-inch-wide green felt
- ¾ yard of 36-inch-wide red or white felt
- Green thread to match felt
- Tacky glue (glue for fabrics)
- 24 adhesive-backed Velcro fasteners (white circles). Before buying these, see Other Ideas, #2, p. 14.
- 1 dowel, ⅝-inch diameter, 26-inch-long
- Felt sheets (8½" × 11") in the following colors and quantities: white (2), red (1), yellow (1), blue (2), brown (1), black (1), purple (1), flesh (1)
- 1 length of cord, ⅛-inch diameter, 36 inches long

Instructions for Making Banner

1. Cut green felt in the shape of a Christmas tree, with the dimensions shown in Figure 1A.

2. Pin tree to red or white background, leaving 5 inches of background above the tree (see Figure 1B).

3. Sew tree to red or white background, using green thread. Stitch around entire perimeter of tree (see Figure 1B).

4. Trace and cut out the patterns on pp. 234-245.

5. Cut out the felt pieces for each of the patterns cut in step 4. Colors and quantities are noted on the patterns.

6. Glue the felt figures onto the appropriate felt circles (e.g., Symbol #23 is a white angel on a blue circle). Pattern pieces indicate which color circle corresponds with each figure.

7. Apply adhesive side of hook (fuzzy) Velcro fasteners to the center of the back of each circle.

8. Apply adhesive side of loop Velcro fasteners to the Christmas tree. Space the fasteners at least four inches apart from each other and at least three inches from the edge of the banner (see Figure 1C).

9. Fold top edge of banner over to the back side 1½ inches (see Figure 1D).

10. Sew overlap 1-inch from fold and ½ inch from edge, as shown in Figure 1E. This forms the casing for the dowel.

11. Drill a hole in the dowel ¾ inch from each end (see Figure 1F). If a drill is not available, use Option 2 in step 13.

12. Insert dowel into casing.

13. *Option 1*
Stiffen ends of cord by wrapping with tape. Draw ends of cord through holes at ends of dowel and knot or tie cord (see Figure 1G).

    Option 2
Tie cord around ends of dowel. Glue cord to dowel so that cord will not slide toward center when hung (see Figure 1H).

Other Ideas

1. Use gold braid, sequins, or other trim to decorate the tree.

2. Instead of using adhesive Velcro, you may want to get regular Velcro and sew it in place. While this is more time-consuming, it is far more durable than the adhesive-back Velcro. If you decide on this option, be sure to sew the Velcro to the back of the felt circles BEFORE gluing the figures on the front of the circles (step 6).

3. It is fairly easy to put the Scripture references on the back of the felt symbols. Buy iron-on laundry marking tape. Using ball-point pen, write down on the tape the Scripture references for each of the Advent family times. Cut tape between references and affix to the back of the corresponding symbols, using procedure indicated on laundry tape package.

4. *Alternative to felt banner*
If you don't have the time or the inclination to make the felt banner, use poster board and construction paper instead. Your children can color or paint the tree, decorating it with glitter, braid, etc., and cut out and glue the symbols onto

Figure 1A

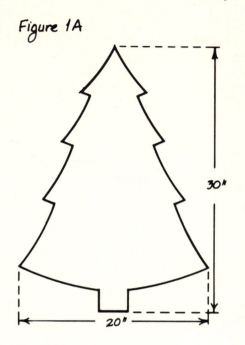

30"

20"

Figure 1B

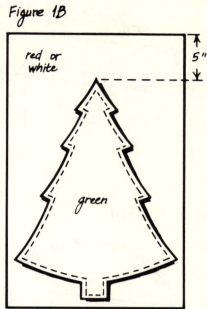

red or white

5"

green

Figure 1C

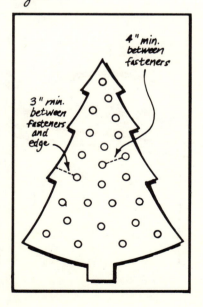

4" min. between fasteners

3" min. between fasteners and edge

Figure 1D

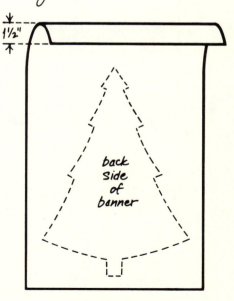

1½"

back side of banner

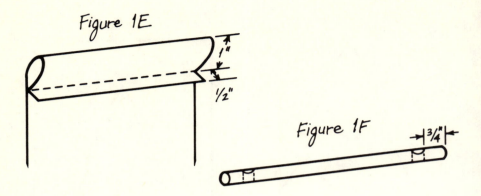

Figure 1E

1"

½"

Figure 1F

¾"

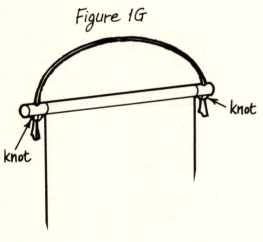

Figure 1G

knot

knot

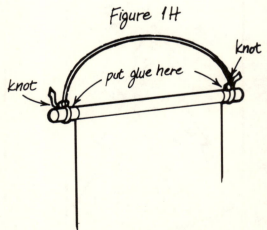

Figure 1H

knot

put glue here

knot

construction paper circles. Then simply tape each symbol to the poster as you go through the Advent family times.

To Use the Advent Banner

1. Keep the felt circles (symbols) in a manila envelope or a zip-lock plastic bag.

2. Before each family time, find the symbol which is indicated for that day's reading.

3. At the conclusion of each family time, allow a child to place the felt symbol on the tree.

The Advent Wreath

Explanation

An Advent Wreath forms an ideal centerpiece around which the family can worship. The glowing flames on the candles remind us of the star of Bethlehem. But more importantly, they remind us of the Light of the World, Jesus Christ. The lighting of the candles calls us to worship and sets this time apart as holy.

The Advent Wreath consists of five candles, four around the circumference of the wreath and one in the center of the wreath. Each candle has a meaning and is lit at a particular time during Advent.

The first candle to be lit, starting with the first Sunday in Advent, is the Prophecy candle. This reminds us that Christ's coming was revealed by God through the prophets hundreds of years before he was born.

The second candle is the Bethlehem candle, pointing to Christ becoming a man in Bethlehem. This is lit in addition to the first candle, starting the second Sunday in Advent.

The third candle joins the first and second on the third Sunday of Advent. This is the Shepherd's candle. With the lighting of this candle, we recognize that we, like the shepherds, must come to Christ, believe in Him, and tell this Good News to others.

The fourth candle, lit with the previous three beginning the fourth Sunday in Advent, is the Angel's candle. With it, we anticipate Christ's Second Coming and focus on His finished work of salvation.

The fifth candle, in the center of the wreath, is the Christ candle. This is lit on Christmas Day. As we light the Christ candle, we recognize that Jesus Christ, the Light of the World, is born this day.

Of the five candles, three are purple, one is rose, and one, white. The purple candles represent Christ's royalty. Purple also represents the attitude of humility and repentance with which we anticipate His coming. The rose candle, the Shepherd's candle, stands for God's love and faithfulness. The white candle in the center symbolizes Christ's holiness and perfection.

As the number of lit candles increases, so we near the celebration of His coming. The ever-increasing brightness heightens our anticipation of this day.

To Make an Advent Wreath

OPTION 1: Purchase an Advent Wreath at a local Christian bookstore. (These are readily available and inexpensive.) Purchase a thicker white candle which can be set in a holder or on a saucer in the center. Decorate the wreath with additional fresh or artificial greens, if desired.

OPTION 2: Purchase a 9-inch aluminum pie plate. Turn it upside down and carefully cut X's in the appropriate locations. Insert the bases of the candles in the X's. Decorate the pie plate with greens.

OPTION 3: Use five small free-standing candle holders. Place four around the outside of a decorated grapevine or styrofoam wreath. Place the fifth candle holder (for the white Christ candle) in the center of the wreath.

To Use the Advent Wreath

Light the appropriate candle(s) at the beginning of each family time. (A parent should do this, for safety reasons.) Each time a new candle is lit (each Sunday during Advent), read and discuss the meaning of that new candle.

At the conclusion of each family time, extinguish the candles. Children may take turns blowing out the candles. Caution should be used at all times.

FAMILY TIMES AROUND GOD'S WORD

December 1: Jesus — Eternal with the Father

Explain:

When Jesus lived on this earth, one of His best friends was named John. After Jesus went up to heaven, John told people about Jesus. Years later, when John was very old, Jesus appeared to John and told him to write down everything Jesus told him. This is one of the things that Jesus said.

Read:
Revelation 22:13

Discuss:

1. Alpha and Omega are the first and last letters of the Greek alphabet, like our A and Z. What did Jesus mean when He said that He is the A and the Z?

2. We began our lives when we started growing within our mothers. Was that true of Jesus? When did He begin?

Memorize:
Revelation 22:13

"I am the Alpha and the Omega, the First and the Last, the Beginning and the End."

Pray:

Lord Jesus, You always were and You always will be. We cannot understand it, but we believe it and give You thanks and praise. In Your name. Amen.

Sing:

"Of the Father's Love Begotten" (*HWC* 118) or "Thou Didst Leave Thy Throne" (*HWC* 127)

Of the Father's love begotten
Ere the worlds began to be,
He is Alpha and Omega,
He the source, the ending He,
Of the things that are, that have been,
And that future years shall see,
Evermore and evermore.

Do:

Find the symbol of the Alpha and Omega. Place this on your Advent Tree.

December 2: Jesus — Eternal with the Father

Explain:

Yesterday we read a verse that was written down by Jesus' friend, John. Today we will read another verse from John's pen, this time from the Gospel of John. John lived with Jesus for three years and watched everything Jesus did. He knew Jesus better than anyone else, most likely. And this is what he said about Jesus.

Read:
John 1:1-2, 14

Discuss:
1. Who is the Word?
2. What do these verses tell us about Him?

Review:
Revelation 22:13

Pray:

Dear Lord, thank You that You are God, yet You came to earth to show us what God is like. We would never have known if You had not been born in Bethlehem that night. Thank you, Lord Jesus. In Jesus' name. Amen.

Sing:
"O Come, All Ye Faithful" (*HWC* 145)

Yea, Lord, we greet Thee,
Born this happy morning,
Jesus, to Thee be glory given;
Word of the Father,
Now in flesh appearing:
O come, let us adore Him,
O come, let us adore Him,
O come, let us adore Him,
Christ, the Lord!

Do:

Find the symbol of the Bible (the Word). Place this on your Advent Tree.

December 3: Jesus — Eternal with the Father

Explain:

So far we've learned that Jesus was with God in the very beginning, long before He was born in Bethlehem. Let's look at something that Jesus did before He came into our world as a baby.

Read:
Colossians 1:15-16

Discuss:
1. What is it that Jesus did?
2. What things did Jesus create?

Review:
Revelation 22:13

Pray:

Lord, You created all things. You are so great. I know that I can trust You because You are the creator and ruler of the universe. In Jesus' name. Amen.

Sing:

"Angels from the Realms of Glory" (*HWC* 131) or "We Come, O Christ, to You" (*HWC* 117)

Angels, from the realms of glory,
Wing your flight o'er all the earth;
Ye, who sang creation's story,
Now proclaim Messiah's birth:
Come and worship, come and worship,
Worship Christ, the newborn King.

Do:

Find the symbol of the planets (creation). Place this on the Advent Tree.

December 4: Jesus — Sent to Save Sinners

Explain:

Yesterday we learned that Jesus made all things. The last and best thing that Jesus made was man. He created Adam and Eve. He made people so that He could love us and we could love Him back. But something happened to cause a problem. Can you guess what that was?

Read:
Isaiah 59:2

Discuss:

1. When you do something wrong or bad, how do your parents feel? What do they do? Why?

2. Ever since Adam and Eve decided to disobey God, we have all sinned and turned away from God. God didn't want us to turn away. He wants us to be close to Him. What do you think He planned to do to take care of this problem?

Memorize:
1 John 4:9

"This is how God showed his love among us: He sent his one and only Son into the world that we might live through him."

Pray:

Dear Lord, I am so sorry for the sins I commit. Thank You that You want to be close to me and You sent Jesus to take away my sin so that I can be close to You forever. In Jesus' name. Amen.

Sing:

"Come, Thou Long-Expected Jesus" (*HWC* 124)

> Come, Thou long-expected Jesus,
> Born to set Thy people free;
> From our fears and sins release us;
> Let us find our rest in Thee.
> Israel's strength and consolation,
> Hope of all the earth Thou art,
> Dear Desire of ev'ry nation,
> Joy of ev'ry longing heart.

Do:

Find the symbol of the black heart. This stands for the sin, or wrong, in our lives. It is because of this sin that Jesus had to come to earth. Place this on the Advent Tree.

December 5: Jesus — Sent to Save Sinners

Explain:

What was the problem that we talked about yesterday? God needed to do something to take care of the problem of our sin so that we could be close to Him again. This verse tells us about what sin is and what God did about it.

Read:

Isaiah 53:6

Discuss:

1. What does this verse tell us about what sin is? Can you give an example?

2. What did God do about our sin?

Review:

1 John 4:9

Pray:

Heavenly Father, thank You so much for sending your Son to take our sin on Himself. He came to be punished in our place. We are sorry for our sin, yet we are so thankful that You loved us enough to die for us. In Jesus' name. Amen.

Sing:

"Good Christian Men, Rejoice" (*HWC* 151)

> Good Christian men, rejoice,
> With heart, and soul, and voice;
> Now ye need not fear the grave:
> Jesus Christ was born to save!
> Calls you one and calls you all
> To gain His everlasting hall.
> Christ was born to save!
> Christ was born to save!

Do:

Find the symbol of the Cross. Jesus came to take the punishment for our sin on the Cross. Place this symbol on the Advent Tree.

December 6: Jesus — Sent to Save Sinners

Explain:

Before Jesus came, God made a way for people's sins to be forgiven. Every year they had to kill (sacrifice) a perfect lamb on an altar. Now this lamb couldn't really take away their sins, but it did show how God would someday send a perfect sacrifice. Killing the lamb was a way to show God that they believed His promise.

The verse that we read today tells us what John the Baptist said when he saw Jesus walking toward him.

Read:

John 1:29

Discuss:

1. Why did John call Jesus the Lamb of God?
2. Why did Jesus leave heaven and come into the world?

Review:

1 John 4:9

Pray:

Thank you so much, Lord Jesus, for coming into the world to take away my sin. In Your name. Amen.

Sing:

"Hark! the Herald Angels Sing" (*HWC* 133)

> Hark! the herald angels sing,
> "Glory to the newborn King:
> Peace on earth, and mercy mild,
> God and sinners reconciled!"
> Joyful, all ye nations, rise,
> Join the triumph of the skies,
> With the angelic host proclaim,
> "Christ is born in Bethlehem."
> Hark, the herald angels sing,
> "Glory to the newborn King!"

Do:

Find the symbol of the lamb. This reminds us that Jesus is the Lamb of God who came to take away the sin of the world. Place this symbol on your Advent Tree.

December 7: Jesus — Sent to Save Sinners

Explain:

When you were a tiny baby, your parents did lots of things to take care of you. They had to get up in the middle of the night and feed you when you cried. They had to watch over you every minute. And when you were sick, they had to hold you and comfort you and sometimes stay up all night with you. It wasn't easy — it was hard work. Why do you think they did these things?

Our heavenly Father loves us, even more than our earthly parents do. This verse tells us how He shows us His love.

Read:

1 John 4:9

Discuss:

1. How did God show us His love?
2. Do you think this was a hard thing to do? Why?

Review:

1 John 4:9

Pray:

Heavenly Father, thank You for Your great love for us. You loved us so much that You did the hardest thing You could do — You gave up Your one and only Son. In His name we pray. Amen.

Sing:

"Thou Didst Leave Thy Throne" (*HWC* 127) or "I Wonder As I Wander" (*HWC* 139)

> Thou didst leave Thy throne and Thy kingly crown
> When Thou camest to earth for me;
> But in Bethlehem's home was there found no room
> For Thy holy nativity.
> O come to my heart, Lord Jesus —
> There is room in my heart for Thee!

Do:

Find the symbol of the red heart. This reminds us of God's love for us — love that cost Him His one and only Son. Place this symbol on the Advent Tree.

December 8: Jesus — Sent to Save Sinners

Explain:

One night, a man named Nicodemus came secretly to ask Jesus some questions. Jesus explained to Nicodemus why God had sent Him into the world.

Read:

John 3:16

Discuss:

1. Why did the Father send Jesus into the world?
2. God loves us so much that He gave us His most precious gift. What do you do with the gifts under the Christmas tree? What do you think God wants us to do with His gift?

Review:

1 John 4:9

Pray:

Thank You for giving us your Son, Jesus, so that we can live forever with You. I thankfully receive Your gift of Jesus as Lord and Savior.

Sing:

"O Little Town of Bethlehem" (*HWC* 141)

> O holy Child of Bethlehem,
> Descend to us, we pray;
> Cast out our sin, and enter in,
> Be born in us today.
> We hear the Christmas angels
> The great glad tidings tell;
> O come to us, abide with us,
> Our Lord Emmanuel! Amen.

Do:

Find the symbol of the gift. This reminds us that Jesus is the greatest gift of all. Place this symbol on your Advent Tree.

December 9: Jesus—Spoken of by the Prophets

Explain:

Before Jesus was born, when God wanted to give His people a message, He would talk to His special helpers. These helpers were called prophets. A prophet would write down God's message, then tell it to the people. One of God's prophets was Isaiah, who lived seven hundred years before Jesus. God told him many things about the Savior that He was going to send.

Read:

Isaiah 9:2

Discuss:

1. What is it like to walk in complete darkness? How is sin like darkness?

2. What does light do to the darkness? Why is Jesus called the light?

Memorize:
Isaiah 9:6

"For to us a child is born, to us a son is given, and the government will be on his shoulders. And he will be called Wonderful Counselor, Mighty God, Everlasting Father, Prince of Peace."

Pray:
Thank You, Lord, that You are perfectly good — there is no sin in You. You are like the light that chases away the darkness of evil. Fill us with Your light and Your goodness, Lord. In Jesus' name. Amen.

Sing:
"Hark! the Herald Angels Sing" (*HWC* 133)

Hail, the heav'n-born Prince of Peace!
Hail, the Sun of Righteousness!
Light and life to all He brings,
Ris'n with healing in His wings.
Mild He lays His glory by,
Born that man no more may die,
Born to raise the sons of earth,
Born to give them second birth.
Hark! the herald angels sing,
"Glory to the newborn King."

Do:
Find the symbol of the candle. This reminds us that Jesus brings light to this dark world. Place this symbol on your Advent Tree.

December 10: Jesus — Spoken of by the Prophets

Explain:
Yesterday we talked about sin being like darkness and Jesus as the light. Here is another message that God gave Isaiah about darkness and light.

Read:
Isaiah 60:1-3

Discuss:

1. Where was the darkness?

2. What does this passage tell us about whom Jesus would come to save?

Review:

Isaiah 9:6

Pray:

Thank You, Lord Jesus, that You came to save people from every nation. Help me to be a light to all the people that I know, by telling them about Your love. In Jesus' name. Amen.

Sing:

"Joy to the World" (*HWC* 125)

> He rules the world with truth and grace,
> And makes the nations prove
> The glories of His righteousness,
> And wonders of His love.

Do:

Find the symbol of the sun. This reminds us that Jesus is the Light of the World. Place this symbol on your Advent Tree.

December 11: Jesus — Spoken of by the Prophets

Explain:

Do you know the name of God's special people? They are called the nation or the children of Israel, or the Jews. They were Abraham's children's children's children (and so on!). Everyone else was called a Gentile. God promised Abraham wonderful things for his family, the Jews. But He also promised Abraham that his family would bring happiness to the whole world. This verse tells how.

Read:

Isaiah 49:6(b)

Discuss:

1. God is talking to those Jews who would believe in Jesus. What did God promise that they would do?

2. God kept His promise. Here we are on the other side of the world two thousand years after Jesus was born — and we have been told about Jesus. Jesus wants us to be a light to people who don't know Him. Whom can you tell about Jesus?

Review:
Isaiah 9:6

Pray:
Dear Lord, You came to save us, and we are so thankful. Help us to show our thankfulness by telling others about You. In Jesus' name. Amen.

Sing:
"Angels from the Realms of Glory" (*HWC* 131)

> Sages, leave your contemplations,
> Brighter visions beam afar;
> Seek the great Desire of nations,
> Ye have seen His natal star:
> Come and worship, come and worship,
> Worship Christ, the newborn King.

Do:
Find the symbol of the trumpet. This reminds us that the Good News of Jesus would be shouted to all the earth. Place this symbol on your Advent Tree.

December 12: Jesus — Spoken of by the Prophets
Explain:
God also told Isaiah what the Savior would be like.

Read:
Isaiah 9:6

Discuss:
1. What do we learn about the Savior from this verse?
2. Tell what each of these names means.

Review:
Isaiah 9:6

Pray:
We praise You, Lord Jesus, that You are the Wonderful Counselor, the Mighty God, the Everlasting Father, and the Prince of Peace. Help me to remember this, and to trust You with my life. In Jesus' name. Amen.

Sing:
"Joy to the World" (*HWC* 125) or "For Unto Us a Child Is Born (*HWC* 146)

> Joy to the world! the Lord is come;
> Let earth receive her King;
> Let every heart prepare Him room,
> And heaven and nature sing.

Do:
Find the symbol of the dove. This reminds us that Jesus is the Prince of Peace. Place this symbol on your Advent Tree.

December 13: Jesus — Spoken of by the Prophets

Explain:
Today's verse follows yesterday's verse about Jesus being the Prince of Peace. It talks about how Jesus rules the world. We actually can't see Jesus on this earth yet, but someday we will. Listen and try to imagine what it will be like.

Read:
Isaiah 9:7

Discuss:
1. What kind of a king is Jesus?

2. If we love and obey Jesus, then He is our king right now. What can you do today to love and obey Jesus?

Review:
Isaiah 9:6

Pray:
Dear Lord, I want You to be my King—every day of my life. Please help me to love and obey You as the King of my life. In Jesus' name. Amen.

Sing:
"What Child Is This?" (*HWC* 137)

> So bring Him incense, gold, and myrrh,
> Come, peasant, King, to own Him;
> The King of Kings salvation brings,
> Let loving hearts enthrone Him.
> This, this is Christ the King,
> Whom shepherds guard and angels sing:
> This, this is Christ the King,
> The Babe, the Son of Mary.

Do:
Find the symbol of the crown. This reminds us that Jesus will rule the world someday as King. If we trust and obey Him, He is our King today. Place this symbol on your Advent Tree.

December 14: Jesus—Spoken of by the Prophets

Explain:
God told Isaiah more about what the Savior would be like.

Read:
Isaiah 40:11

Discuss:
1. Who is the Shepherd? Who is the flock?
2. What do we learn about what the Savior would be like? Was Jesus like this?
3. How does Jesus care for you like a shepherd?

Review:
Isaiah 9:6

Pray:
Dear Jesus, You are so gentle and kind to us. Thank You for loving us and caring for us like a shepherd. In Your name we pray. Amen.

Sing:
"Savior, Like a Shepherd Lead Us" (*HWC* 462) or "Away in a Manger" (*HWC* 157)

> Savior, like a Shepherd lead us,
> Much we need Thy tender care;
> In Thy pleasant pastures feed us,
> For our use Thy folds prepare:
> Blessed Jesus, blessed Jesus,
> Thou has bought us, Thine we are.

Do:
Find the symbol of the shepherd's staff. This reminds us that Jesus is the Good Shepherd. Place this symbol on the Advent Tree.

December 15: Jesus—Spoken of by the Prophets

Explain:
Do you remember Israel's greatest king, King David? David was the son of Jesse. In these verses, God promises that the Savior will come from David's (and Jesse's) family. Remember, we learned that He would sit on David's throne.

Read:
Isaiah 11:1-3

Discuss:
1. Jesus was the Branch that would come from the stump or family of David. Matthew 1 and Luke 3:23-31 show that Jesus did come from David's family. What does this tell us about how God keeps His promises?
2. What else does this verse tell us about what Jesus would be like?

Review:
Isaiah 9:6

Pray:
Heavenly Father, thank You for keeping all Your promises. And thank You that Jesus knew everything and happily obeyed You. Help me to happily obey You today, Lord. In Jesus' name. Amen.

Sing:
"Lo! How a Rose E'er Blooming" (*HWC* 160)

> Lo, how a Rose e'er blooming
> From tender stem hath sprung!
> Of Jesse's lineage coming
> As men of old have sung.
> It came, a Flower bright,
> Amid the cold of winter,
> When half-gone was the night.
>
> This Flower, whose fragrance tender
> With sweetness fills the air,
> Dispels with glorious splendor
> The darkness everywhere.
> True man, yet very God,
> From sin and death He saves us
> And lightens every load.

Do:
Find the symbol of the stump and the branch. The stump is the family of Jesse and David. Jesus is the Branch that grew out of this family, just as God promised. Place this symbol on the Advent Tree.

December 16: Jesus — Spoken of by the Prophets

Explain:
God told the prophet Micah where the Savior would be born.

Read:
Micah 5:2

Discuss:

1. God is talking to the little village of Bethlehem. What message does He have for Bethlehem?

2. Where was Jesus born? Why was He born there — did Mary live there? God had it all planned out. Read Luke 2:1-4.

Review:
Isaiah 9:6

Pray:

Thank You, Lord, that You planned every little detail of how and where Jesus would be born. Nothing happened by accident. You are a great and wonderful God. We praise You in Jesus' name. Amen.

Sing:
"O Little Town of Bethlehem" (*HWC* 141)

> O little town of Bethlehem,
> How still we see thee lie!
> Above thy deep and dreamless sleep
> The silent stars go by;
> Yet in thy dark streets shineth
> The everlasting Light;
> The hopes and fears of all the years
> Are met in thee tonight.

Do:

Find the symbol of the Bethlehem building. This reminds us that Jesus was born in Bethlehem, just as God had said many years before. Place this symbol on your Advent Tree.

December 17: Jesus — Spoken of by the Prophets

Explain:

Here God tells Isaiah about the birth of this Savior that would come seven hundred years later.

Read:
Isaiah 7:14

Discuss:
1. What would this special baby boy be called?
2. Emmanuel means "God with us." How does this name fit Jesus? (Read Luke 1:32.)

Review:
Isaiah 9:6

Pray:
How wonderful You are, Lord! Thank You for coming to earth to be one of us! In Jesus' name. Amen.

Sing:
"O Come, O Come, Emmanuel" (*HWC* 123)

> O come, O come, Emmanuel,
> And ransom captive Israel,
> That mourns in lonely exile here,
> Until the Son of God appear.
> Rejoice! Rejoice! Emmanuel
> Shall come to thee, O Israel!

Do:
Find the symbol of the manger. This reminds us of the miracle of Jesus' birth, as the prophets foretold. Place this symbol on your Advent Tree.

December 18: Jesus — Born of the Virgin Mary
Explain:
Just as God promised, He chose a young woman to be the mother of His own Son. What was her name? God told her about this special job by sending His angel Gabriel.

Read:
Luke 1:26-38

Discuss:
1. What message did Gabriel bring to Mary? How would you feel if you were Mary?
2. What did Mary say?

Memorize:

Luke 1:37

"For nothing is impossible with God."

Pray:

Dear Lord, nothing is impossible for You. Help me obey You as Mary did. Help me not to be afraid but simply to trust and obey You. In Jesus' name. Amen.

Sing:

"Lo! How a Rose E'er Blooming" (*HWC* 160) or "Silent Night" (*HWC* 147)

> Isaiah 'twas foretold it,
> The Rose I have in mind;
> With Mary we behold it,
> The virgin mother kind.
> To show God's love aright
> She bore to men a Savior,
> When half-gone was the night.

Do:

Find the symbol of Mary, Jesus' mother. Place this symbol on your Advent Tree.

December 19: Jesus — Born of the Virgin Mary

Explain:

Do you know what your name means? In the Bible, names were very important. They usually meant something. They stood for who the person was and what he would do.

Before Jesus was born, God sent His angel Gabriel to Joseph. Gabriel told Joseph what the baby should be named.

Read:

Matthew 1:20-24

Discuss:

1. What reason did the angel give for naming the baby Jesus?
2. Jesus means "The Lord saves." Why does this name fit Jesus?

Review:
Luke 1:37

Pray:
We are so thankful that You came to save us, Lord Jesus. In Your name. Amen.

Sing:
"Good Christian Men, Rejoice!" (*HWC* 151)

> Good Christian men, rejoice,
> With heart, and soul, and voice;
> Now ye need not fear the grave:
> Jesus Christ was born to save!
> Calls you one and calls you all
> To gain His everlasting hall.
> Christ was born to save!
> Christ was born to save!

Do:
Find the symbol of Joseph. Place this symbol on your Advent Tree.

December 20: Jesus — Born of the Virgin Mary

Explain:
These are verses that you have heard many times. This time, close your eyes and try to imagine what it was like for Mary and Joseph. How did they feel? What did they see, hear, and smell around them?

Read:
Luke 2:1-7

Discuss:
1. What was it like for Mary and Joseph that night?
2. If you were God and could pick where your Son would be born, would you have picked this poor family who had nowhere to stay? Why do you think God chose to become poor and homeless instead of rich?

Review:
Luke 1:37

Pray:
Thank You, Lord, that You care for poor people, people who have no homes and nowhere to go. You know what it is like, don't You, Lord? Show me what I can do to help poor people, too, Lord. In Jesus' name. Amen.

Sing:
"What Child Is This?" (*HWC* 137)

> What child is this, who, laid to rest,
> On Mary's lap is sleeping?
> Whom angels greet with anthems sweet,
> While shepherds watch are keeping?
> This, this is Christ the King,
> Whom shepherds guard and angels sing;
> This, this is Christ the King,
> The Babe, the son of Mary.
>
> Why lies He in such mean estate
> Where ox and ass are feeding?
> Good Christian, fear; for sinners here
> The silent Word is pleading.
> This, this is Christ the King,
> Whom shepherds guard and angels sing;
> This, this is Christ the King,
> The Babe, the son of Mary.

Do:
Find the symbol of the baby Jesus. Place this symbol on your Advent Tree.

December 21: Jesus—Born of the Virgin Mary

Explain:
Count how many times angels appeared to people around the time of Jesus' birth. The Bible doesn't tell us of any angels appearing or prophets speaking for the four hundred years before this time. Why, all of a sudden, were all these angels appearing?

Read:
Luke 2:8-14

Discuss:
1. Describe what the shepherds saw that night.
2. Shepherds were not considered important people. Why do you think God sent His angels to these poor shepherds?

Memorize:
Luke 2:12

"This will be a sign to you: You will find a baby wrapped in cloths and lying in a manger."

Pray:
Thank You, Lord, that everyone is important to You—even poor, simple shepherds. Thank You that no matter how rich, smart or important I am or am not, You came to save me from my sins. In Jesus' name. Amen.

Sing:
"Angels We Have Heard on High" (*HWC* 132) or "Go Tell It on the Mountain" (*HWC* 138)

> Angels we have heard on high,
> Sweetly singing o'er the plains,
> And the mountains in reply
> Echo back their joyous strains.
> Gloria in excelsis Deo.
>
> Shepherds, why this jubilee?
> Why your joyous strains prolong?
> Say what may the tidings be,
> Which inspire your heav'nly song?
> Gloria in excelsis Deo.

Do:
Find the symbol of the angel. This reminds us of the angels who came to announce Jesus' birth to the shepherds. Place this symbol on your Advent tree.

December 22: Jesus—Born of the Virgin Mary

Explain:

After the angels disappeared, the shepherds didn't just say, "Wasn't that a nice concert?" They were excited! Let's see what they did . . .

Read:
Luke 2:15-20

Discuss:

1. What did the shepherds want to do? What did they do after they saw Jesus?

2. You, too, have met Jesus. You see Him each day as you read His Word, the Bible, and as you pray to Him. Do you get excited about Him? Whom can you tell about Jesus this week?

Review:
Luke 2:12

Pray:

Thank You, Lord, that we can see You and worship You, just as the shepherds did. Help me to be excited about knowing You. Help me to tell my friends about all the good things You have done. In Jesus' name. Amen.

Sing:
"Angels We Have Heard on High" (*HWC* 132)

> Come to Bethlehem, and see
> Him whose birth the angels sing;
> Come adore on bended knee
> Christ the Lord, the newborn King.
> Gloria in excelsis Deo.
>
> See within a manger laid
> Jesus, Lord of heav'n and earth!
> Mary, Joseph, lend your aid,
> With us sing our Savior's birth.
> Gloria in excelsis Deo.

Do:

Find the symbol of the musical notes. This reminds us that the shepherds went on their way praising God and telling others about what they had seen. Place this symbol on your Advent Tree.

December 23: Jesus — Born of the Virgin Mary

Explain:

The wise men who followed the star were not kings — they were men who studied the stars. We don't know how many wise men there were; the Bible doesn't say. See what you can figure out about these wise men.

Read:

Matthew 2:1-8

Discuss:

1. Why were the wise men looking for the newborn king?

2. Herod was a wicked man who was the king of the Jews at that time. Why did he want to find Jesus?

Review:

Luke 2:12

Pray:

Dear Lord, I want to be like the wise men. They looked for You so that they could worship You. Help me to do this each day. In Jesus' name. Amen.

Sing:

"As With Gladness Men of Old" (*HWC* 163) or "O Holy Night!" (*HWC* 148)

> As with gladness men of old
> Did the guiding star behold;
> As with joy they hailed its light,
> Leading onward, beaming bright;
> So, most gracious Lord, may we
> Evermore be led to Thee.

Do:

Find the symbol of the star. This represents the star that led the wise men to the Christ child. Place this symbol on your Advent Tree.

December 24: Jesus — Born of the Virgin Mary

Explain:

Each of the gifts that the wise men brought has a special meaning. Gold stood for the riches of a king. Jesus would be King of kings. Incense was used by priests in temple worship. Jesus would be our high priest who would represent us to the Father. Myrrh was a perfume put on dead people. Jesus would die as the perfect sacrifice for our sins. The wise men's gifts showed that Jesus would be King, Priest, and Sacrifice.

Read:

Matthew 2:9-12

Discuss:

1. What do these verses tell us about the wise men? Why did they bring Jesus gifts?

2. What gift can you give to Jesus tonight?

Review:

Luke 2:12

Pray:

Dear Lord, You gave Your life for me. Nothing I could give You could ever repay You. But I know that You want me to give You my life. So this Christmas, Lord, I give You my heart — all that I am and have is Yours. In Jesus' name. Amen.

Sing:

"As With Gladness Men of Old" (*HWC* 163) or "We Three Kings" (*HWC* 166)

> As they offered gifts most rare
> At that manger rude and bare;

So may we with holy joy,
Pure and free from sin's alloy,
All our costliest treasures bring,
Christ, to Thee, our heavenly King. Amen.

Do:

Find the symbol of the wise men's gifts. Place this symbol on your Advent Tree.

FAMILY CELEBRATION

Two family celebrations are included in the Christmas season. The first is a format for family worship on Christmas. This can be celebrated either Christmas Eve or Christmas Day, according to your family tradition. The second celebration is a Twelfth Night party for Epiphany, a festive conclusion to the Christmas season.

Family Worship at Christmas

Leader:

"My soul glorifies the Lord and my spirit rejoices in God my Savior" (Luke 1:46b-47).

Sing:

"O Come, All Ye Faithful" (*HWC* 145)

Yea, Lord, we greet Thee,
Born this happy morning,
Jesus, to Thee be glory given;
Word of the Father,
Now in flesh appearing:
O come, let us adore Him,
O come, let us adore Him,
O come, let us adore Him,
Christ, the Lord!

Read:
Isaiah 9:2-7

Sing:

"Joy to the World" (*HWC* 125)

> Joy to the world! the Lord is come;
> Let earth receive her King;
> Let every heart prepare Him room,
> And heaven and nature sing.
>
> Joy to the world! the Savior reigns;
> Let men their songs employ,
> While fields and floods, rocks, hills and plains
> Repeat the sounding joy.
>
> He rules the world with truth and grace,
> And makes the nations prove
> The glories of His righteousness,
> And wonders of His love.

Read:

Luke 2:1-20

Sing:

"Silent Night" (*HWC* 147)

> Silent night, holy night,
> All is calm, all is bright
> Round yon Virgin Mother and Child.
> Holy Infant, so tender and mild,
> Sleep in heavenly peace.
>
> Silent night, holy night,
> Shepherds quake at the sight;
> Glories stream from heaven afar,
> Heavenly hosts sing, Alleluia,
> Christ, the Savior, is born!
>
> Silent night, holy night,
> Son of God, love's pure light
> Radiant beams from thy holy face,
> With the dawn of redeeming grace,
> Jesus, Lord, at thy birth.

Read:

Galatians 4:4-7

Sing:

"Hark, the Herald Angels Sing" (*HWC* 133)

> Hark! the herald angels sing,
> "Glory to the newborn King:
> Peace on earth, and mercy mild,
> God and sinners reconciled!"
> Joyful, all ye nations, rise,
> Join the triumph of the skies,
> With the angelic host proclaim,
> "Christ is born in Bethlehem."
> Hark, the herald angels sing,
> "Glory to the newborn King!"
>
> Christ, by highest heaven adored,
> Christ, the everlasting Lord,
> Late in time behold him come,
> Offspring of a Virgin's womb.
> Veiled in flesh the Godhead see;
> Hail, the incarnate Deity,
> Pleased as Man with man to dwell,
> Jesus, our Emmanuel!

Discuss:

1. Why did God send His Son?

2. These verses tell us that if we have accepted God's gift of His Son Jesus, we are His own children. What does it say that we call God? (*Abba* means *Daddy*.)

3. An heir is a son who gets what belonged to his father. What belongs to God? What does God give us?

Pray:

Thank You, Father, for the greatest gift of all — Your Son, Our Savior, Jesus Christ the Lord.

Respond:

Glory to God in the Highest, and on earth peace to men on whom His favor rests!

Twelfth Night Party

A modern-day celebration of Epiphany offers many advantages. The party can be planned and enjoyed in the relaxation of the post-Christmas season. It allows one final opportunity to sing all the favorite Christmas carols and recall all the beautiful Scriptures of Advent. Most important, it reiterates the spiritual significance of Christ's coming in a way that is memorable to our children.

This is a celebration that can be enjoyed by your family alone, but it is more fun with lots of people. So try to invite family and friends to this festive occasion. If everyone brings a part of the meal, the burden of preparation and cost is shared.

This party embodies three elements: (1) the feast, (2) the pageant, and (3) the service.

Preparation

Invite family and friends to this Feast of Lights. If everyone brings a dish to share, the preparations are minimal.

Aside from the meal, here are the things you will need to celebrate this festival:

1. Costumes and props for the children's reenactment of the Christmas story. These can be make-shift. Let the children help assemble them.

2. Hymn books or song sheets with the words to all the Christmas carols.

3. Your Advent Tree, still decorated with all the symbols.

4. The verses from the Advent family times written out on slips of paper.

The Feast

Before the festive meal is eaten, read 2 Corinthians 4:6. Briefly explain that Epiphany or the Feast of Lights celebrates God's showing Himself to us in the person of Jesus Christ. Offer a prayer of worship and thanksgiving.

The Pageant

As the adults are finishing the meal, the children (long since down from the table, no doubt) may don costumes and prepare to reenact the events of Christ's birth. This production can be left entirely to the children if they are school-age. (Pre-schoolers will need help and prompting.) Their interpretation of the Biblical account is sure to entertain the adults as well as reinforce the facts of the stories in the minds of the children.

The Service

After the pageant, it is time for the "service" of undecorating the Advent Tree. Pass out hymn books or song sheets and the slips of paper with the verses written on them. Children too young to read verses may participate by taking symbols off the Advent Tree.

First, light candles around the room (taking every safety precaution, of course) and offer a prayer of praise to Christ, the Light of the World. Remind everyone that tonight we celebrate the wise men following the light of the star to find the true Light of the World.

Beginning with the first symbol (the Alpha and Omega), have a child, or several children, remove each symbol from the tree, one at a time, while someone reads the corresponding verse or passage. Between the Scripture readings, sing together suitable Christmas carols. Proceed through the twenty-four days of Advent until the tree stands barren.

Conclude with a time of conversational prayer, praising and thanking God for His great gift, His Son.

Love bade me welcome; yet my soul drew back,
    Guilty of dust and sin.
But quick-eyed Love, observing me grow slack
    From my first entrance in,
Drew nearer to me, sweetly questioning
    If I lacked anything.

"A guest," I answered, "worthy to be here."
    Love said, "You shall be he."
"I, the unkind, ungrateful? Ah, my dear,
    I cannot look on Thee."
Love took my hand, and smiling, did reply,
    "Who made the eyes but I?"

"Truth, Lord, but I have marred them, let my shame
    Go where it doth deserve."
"And know you not," says Love,
    "who bore the blame?"
"My dear, then I will serve."
"You must sit down," says Love,
    "and taste my meat."
    So I did sit and eat.

George Herbert, 1593-1633
Love (3)

GOD'S KIND
OF LOVE

Valentine's Day

The Roman soldiers pushed the pastor roughly out the door of the prison into the dawn-washed courtyard. Valentine stood, blinking, as his eyes grew accustomed to the early morning light. It seemed that he had been in that dark prison cell forever. He took a deep breath of the fresh air. It was tinged with a hint of spring. High overhead pairs of birds circled and called to one another. Life beckoned, but he could not answer its call.

Another rough push propelled him toward the center of the courtyard where death awaited him. It was a simple but gruesome instrument, a large, heavy axe. As Valentine proceeded toward the block, the courtyard seemed to fill with familiar faces. He saw the tattered forms of poor people to whom he had ministered. Radiant faces called words of encouragement, faces of those whose sicknesses had been healed by Valentine's gentle care. And all around he recognized individuals who had come to Christ through his faithful witness. He would see them again someday, robed in white, free from the pain and persecution of this earthly life.

The faces vanished. Valentine stood alone before the block, flanked by the soldiers who would administer his sentence. He knelt silently, thinking only of the face he soon would see, the face of his Savior, the Lamb of God.

INTRODUCTION

Background

Valentine, a pastor and physician in Rome, was beheaded by order of Claudius the Goth in 269 A.D. It is his life and death for Christ that we commemorate on February 14.

The celebration of romantic love actually has nothing to do with St. Valentine. This aspect of Valentine's Day was added later as a result of the belief that birds mated on February 14. This day came to be associated with lovers and courting couples.

While there certainly is a place for romantic love in God's scheme of things, it cannot compare to the love that Valentine's life exemplified. His sacrificial love mirrors the ultimate love, the love that God showed toward us when He gave His Son as a sacrifice for our sins.

Overview

Christian families may take this celebration of love as an opportunity to explore what God's Word says about love. The world identifies physical attraction as love. God's Word gives us a much higher standard. God's kind of love puts the other person's interests before one's own. It involves commitment, commitment that stands the test of time. It is not contingent on the other person's response but continues giving regardless of the response.

We will take the three weeks before Valentine's day to look at several examples of God's kind of love. The first family time will emphasize the unselfish nature of love by looking at the commitment of Ruth to Naomi. David's commitment to Jonathan is the subject of the second family time. The focus of this lesson is on keeping one's promises.

Jesus showed us God's kind of love, both in His life and death and in His teaching. For the last two family times, we will look at two of Jesus' parables that sketch pictures of perfect love. The parable of the Prodigal Son (better named the parable of the loving father) describes God's unconditional love for sinners and His forgiveness for those who turn to Him. The parable of the Good Samaritan shows us that true love for God is demonstrated in acts of love and mercy for those in need.

FAMILY PROJECT

The family project, a Valentine Tree, is designed to underscore what the Bible says about love by requiring each person to act on what he has learned. Each member of the family will make four Valentine hearts, one for each family time before Valentine's Day. After the Bible discussion, there is an opportunity to write down on the hearts how you will apply the lesson to your life. Each person will think of one thing that he will do that week to demonstrate God's kind of love. Only when he has acted on it, can the family member hang his heart on the Valentine tree. By Valentine's Day, the tree should be full of paper hearts, representing many acts of love and kindness.

The family activity is a Valentine's Day party that is a celebration of God's kind of love. The only preparation necessary is the preparation of a nice meal. Both the special dinner and the activity that follows highlight our love for one another and God's love that binds us together and draws us to Him.

Valentine's Day Tree

Materials

- One tree branch (lightweight, but with lots of small branches)
- One pot or vase for holding tree branch
- Soil or rocks for weighting down pot or vase
- Pink, white, and red construction paper
- Paper doilies
- White yarn
- Scissors
- Glue
- Paper punch
- Optional:
  - Glitter
  - Crayons
  - Tempera or water color paints

Instructions

1. Set tree branch in pot or vase. Support the tree branch by filling the vase or pot with soil or rocks. This will be your family Valentine Tree.

2. Put the Valentine Tree in an appropriate place (away from little fingers, but somewhere all can see it).

3. Cut hearts out of the pink, white, and red construction paper. These need to be large enough to have five or six words written on them. Each person in the family will need at least four hearts.

4. Have each person decorate his or her own hearts. Use doilies, construction paper, and the like. Encourage creativity.

5. Punch a hole at the top of each heart.

6. Cut a 6-inch length of yarn for each heart.

7. Thread the yarn through the hole and tie the ends of the yarn together in a secure knot. This yarn loop will be used to hang the heart on the Valentine Tree.

8. After the glue, paint, and the like dry, place the hearts in a folder or manila envelope and keep them with this book and your Bible. They will be used during the family times preceding Valentine's Day.

Using the Valentine Tree

Each of the four family times during the Valentine season includes a special "action item." This is an action that each person should take in response to the Bible discussion. Usually it is an act of kindness.

At the appropriate time, the parent will hand each person one of the hearts that that person made. Each family member will write down on his or her heart the action that he or she will take. (Parents will write for younger children, of course. Make sure that the action is the child's own idea, however.)

After family time, each person will hang the heart somewhere in his or her own room. This will be a reminder to follow through with the action. When each person has done a loving deed, the heart may be hung on the Valentine Tree.

By Valentine's Day, the tree should be full of pink, white, and red paper hearts. More important, your family's hearts should be filled with the joy that comes from obeying God and showing His love to others.

FAMILY TIMES
AROUND GOD'S WORD

**Three Weeks before
Valentine's Day**

Naomi and Ruth: An Unselfish Love

Explain:

Do you know what a famine is? That is when there is no food in a land. What would you do if there were a continuing famine in our country? You'd probably move to a place where there was enough food to eat. That's what Naomi, her husband, and her two sons did long ago in the land of Israel. They moved to a nearby country called Moab.

Then a sad thing happened—Naomi's husband died. Naomi's sons married women from Moab—their names were Orpah and Ruth. Naomi and her two sons and their wives lived in Moab for ten years. Then another very sad thing happened. Both Naomi's sons died. Now Naomi had no family left at all, except for Orpah and Ruth.

When the famine in Israel was over, Naomi decided to move back to her home.

Read:
Ruth 1:6-18

Discuss:

1. Did Naomi's daughters-in-law love her? How do you know?

2. Which one loved her more? How do you know?

3. What did Ruth leave in order to be with Naomi?

4. Ruth gave up everything for Naomi. How was her love for Naomi like Jesus' love for us?

5. Ruth was unselfish. That means she wasn't thinking of herself and what would make her happy. Instead she thought of Naomi and what would be best for her. Can you think of ways that you can be unselfish with your family?

Do:

Write down on a heart one unselfish thing you can do for someone in your family this week. Hang the heart in your room to remind you. When you have done your unselfish act, you may hang your heart on the Valentine tree.

Memorize:

John 15:13

"Greater love has no one than this, that one lay down his life for his friends."

Pray:

Dear Lord, You left all the riches of heaven to come down and save us. Help us to be unselfish, too, in our love for other people. In Jesus' name. Amen.

Sing:

"Jesus, Priceless Treasure" (*HWC* 413) or "What Wondrous Love is This?" (*HWC* 177) or "O Love That Will Not Let Me Go" (*HWC* 374)

> Jesus, priceless Treasure,
> Source of purest pleasure,
> Truest friend to me;
> Long my heart hath panted,
> 'Til it well nigh fainted,
> Thirsting after Thee.
> Thine I am, O spotless Lamb,
> I will suffer nought to hide Thee,
> Ask for nought beside Thee.

Two Weeks before Valentine's Day

David and Jonathan: A Promise Kept

Explain:

Remember the story of David and Goliath? David was just a young shepherd boy at the time. The king was Saul, the first king of Israel. When Saul started to disobey God, God decided that someday David would be king instead. This made Saul hate David.

But Saul had a son named Jonathan who was David's best friend in the whole world. One day Jonathan found out that his father meant to kill David. Jonathan told David about Saul's plans so that David could run away and hide from Saul. David and Jonathan both cried as they said goodbye for the last time. But before David went he promised Jonathan that he would always be kind to Jonathan and his family (1 Samuel 20). David never saw his friend Jonathan again. Jonathan and Saul were killed in a war, and David became the king. David didn't know that Jonathan had a son who was still alive.

Read:

2 Samuel 4:4 and 2 Samuel 9:1-13

(Try acting out this action-packed story. You may want to include 1 Samuel 20 in your skit.)

Discuss:

1. How did Mephibosheth become crippled? How old was he then?

2. When David found out about Mephibosheth, the little son of Jonathan had grown up. He even had a young son of his own. Why did David want to find Mephibosheth?

3. What did David do for Mephibosheth? Did he keep his promise to Jonathan?

4. What lessons about love and friendship does this story teach you? Do you think it's important to keep your promises? Why?

Do:

Write on one of the hearts a promise that you plan to keep this week. Hang the heart somewhere in your room to help you remember. Then, when you have kept your promise, hang your heart on the Valentine Tree.

Memorize:

1 John 3:16

"This is how we know what love is: Jesus Christ laid down his life for us. And we ought to lay down our lives for our brothers."

Pray:

Dear Father, You showed us what love really is by sending Jesus to die for us. Help us to show love to other people by being kind and by keeping our promises. In Jesus' name. Amen.

Sing:

"The King of Love My Shepherd Is" (*HWC* 468) or "Standing on the Promises" (*HWC* 271) or "My Hope is Built on Nothing Less" (*HWC* 404)

> The King of love my Shepherd is,
> Whose goodness faileth never;
> I nothing lack if I am His,
> And He is mine for ever.
>
> Perverse and foolish oft I strayed,
> But yet in love He sought me,
> And on His shoulder gently laid,
> And home, rejoicing, brought me.

One Week before Valentine's Day

The Parable of the Loving Father

Explain:

Don't you love a good story? Jesus told lots of stories. He told stories to teach people about many important things. Today we will read one of Jesus' stories. He told this story after some people got mad at Him. They didn't like how nice Jesus was to people who had done many bad things. They didn't understand that God loves people with a special kind of love.

Read:

Luke 15:11-24

Discuss:

1. The young son asked his dad to give him the money that would belong to him when his dad died. Why did he want the money? What did he do with all his dad's money?

2. How do you think this made his father feel? Did his dad get angry and decide he didn't love the son anymore? How do you know?

3. Why did the son come home? How did the father feel when he saw his son coming? What did he do?

4. Jesus wanted the people to know how happy God is when we are sorry for our sin. It doesn't matter what bad things we have done or how many times we've done them. God loves us and forgives us and welcomes us home. Think of some words that describe what God is like.

Do:

Think of something kind you can make or do for someone this week. Write it down on one of your hearts. Hang it on the tree when you have done your kind action.

Memorize:

Romans 5:8

"But God demonstrates his own love for us in this: While we were still sinners, Christ died for us."

Pray:

Your love is perfect, heavenly Father. You loved us before we loved You. And when we are sorry for our sins, You always forgive us. You never stop loving us. Thank You for Your love. Help us to love others with Your special kind of love. In Jesus' name. Amen.

Sing:

"Just As I Am" (*HWC* 342) or "There's a Wideness in God's Mercy" (*HWC* 68) or "Children of the Heavenly Father" (*HWC* 44)

> Just As I am, without one plea,
> But that Thy Blood was shed for me,
> And that Thou bidd'st me come to Thee,
> O Lamb of God, I come, I come.
>
> Just as I am, Thou wilt receive
> Wilt welcome, pardon, cleanse, relieve;
> Because Thy promise I believe,
> O Lamb of God, I come, I come.

The Week of Valentine's Day

The Good Samaritan

Explain:

Mark Twain once said that it wasn't what he didn't understand about the Bible that bothered him. What bothered him was the part he did understand.

In today's story, Jesus is questioned by a man who thinks he knows all the answers. Jesus tells a story (a parable) to show him that loving God isn't a matter of knowing all the answers. We love God by doing what He says. And that isn't always easy.

Read:
Luke 10:25-37

Discuss:

1. What happened to the man who was traveling? How do you think he felt?

2. Priests and Levites were men who spent all their time studying the Bible. They knew all about God. Do you think these two men loved God? Why or why not?

3. The man who was hurt was a Jew. Most Jews hated Samaritans. Samaritans were different. They looked different and they even worshiped God differently. Jews thought that Samaritans weren't nearly as good as they were. Do you think that was true? What did this Samaritan do? How did he show that he loved God?

4. Sometimes the people who say unkind things to us are the people who need God's love the most. Can you think of someone like that? What can you do to show them God's love?

Do:

Write this down on a heart, then hang the heart on the Valentine tree when you have done it.

Memorize:
Luke 10:27

"He answered: 'Love the Lord your God with all your heart and with all your soul and with all your strength and with all your mind'; and, 'Love your neighbor as yourself.'"

Pray:

Father, we don't want to be like the priest or the Levite in this story. We want to be like the Samaritan. Help us to notice the people around us who need Your love. And help us to show them Your love and kindness. In Jesus' name. Amen.

Sing:

"Take My Life and Let It Be" (*HWC* 379) or "Spirit of God, Descend Upon My Heart" (*HWC* 249)

> Take my life, and let it be
> Consecrated, Lord, to Thee
> Take my moments and my days,
> Let them flow in ceaseless praise.
>
> Take my hands, and let them move
> At the impulse of thy love;
> Take my feet, and let them be
> Swift and beautiful for Thee.
>
> Take my love; my Lord, I pour
> At Thy feet its treasure-store;
> Take myself, and I will be
> Ever, only, all for Thee.

FAMILY CELEBRATION

A Valentine's Day party is a special way of saying "I love you" to all the members of your family. You may want to include relatives or good family friends in this event. This party includes a dinner and a fun after-dinner game, called "Whom Do I Love?"

Valentine's Day Dinner

Prepare one of your family's favorite meals. Include the entire family in the preparations. It should be everyone's labor of love, not just Mom's. Bring out the linen tablecloth and the good china. Candlelight and a lovely table are one way to say "You're special" to the members of your family.

The prayer before the meal can be a time of thanksgiving for the loving relationships in your family. Hold hands around the table and let everyone contribute a short prayer of thanksgiving for the family, and for God's love.

During the meal, recall all that your family has learned about love in the preceding weeks. Ask everyone to share what was most meaningful to him or her. If you have guests, you can explain to them what the true meaning of Valentine's Day is. Describe for them God's kind of love.

Valentine's Day Activity
"Whom Do I Love?"
Number of Players:
4-20

Length of Time:
10-20 minutes

Materials:
Clock or watch with second hand

Object of Game:
To communicate nonverbally the identity of one of your family members.

To Play:
This game is a variation on charades. Each person takes a turn being an actor. The actor chooses one person in the room whose identity he will try to communicate without words. He will do this by acting out things that that person does or hobbies that the person enjoys.

The actor begins by saying, "Whom do I love?" The actor then has one minute to depict the identity of the other person. Participants call out their guesses by saying, "You love so-and-so!" The person with the right answer takes the next turn unless he has already had a turn. If so, he may give the turn to a person who has not yet had a turn.

Variation:

To make the game longer or more difficult, try characterizing Bible characters. Instead of saying, "Whom do I love?" begin the one-minute characterization by saying, "Whom does God love?" Then pantomime a scenario from the life of a Bible character. You may need to increase the amount of time from one minute to three minutes for each characterization.

Lord, who created man in wealth and store,
Though foolishly he lost the same,
Decaying more and more
Till he became
Most poor:
With these
O let me rise
As larks, harmoniously,
And sing this day thy victories —
Then shall the fall further the flight in me.

George Herbert, 1593-1633
from Easter Wings

THREE

THE ROAD
TO CALVARY

Easter

The brightness of the noonday sun did little to mitigate the darkness of their spirits. Depression had settled over them like a thick fog, clouding their senses. It had taken every ounce of their energy to gather together their belongings and to set out on their short homeward trek to Emmaus.

"I don't understand it!" Rachel repeated for the hundredth time. "I was sure that He was the Messiah. Who else could do such miracles? Who else spoke as He did—with the authority of the Lord Himself?"

"I don't know," returned Cleopas dumbly, his face cast down. He felt as if his heart were broken and he would never recover. Cleopas hardly noticed when a fellow traveler overtook them.

"You look very serious, my friends," the stranger remarked. "What have you been discussing as you walk along?"

The man and wife stopped and turned to the newcomer, who read pain in their faces.

"Are you just visiting Jerusalem? Don't you know about the things that have happened there the past few days?" Cleopas asked.

"What things?"

It was as if the stranger had opened the floodgates. The story poured forth from the two disciples. They described the trial and crucifixion of their Master, Jesus of Nazareth, and their deep disappointment in how things had turned out. Even more confusing were reports that the body was missing.

The stranger's response shocked them.

"How foolish you are! Don't you believe all that the prophets have spoken? Didn't Messiah have to suffer these things before entering His glory?"

This sharp rebuke, like a dousing of cold water, awakened them from their despondency.

The stranger went on to explain the Scriptures to them. He began with the books of Moses and made His way through all the prophets. Clearly He showed them that Jesus of Nazareth was the one to whom all the Scriptures pointed. Cleopas and Rachel began to see that even the horrendous events of Passover week were part of God's eternal plan.

Before they knew it, they had reached their destination. The hours had passed like moments as they had listened, enrapt, to their unusual friend. Now they were reluctant to let Him go.

"Please come and stay with us," Rachel urged.

"It is nearly evening — the day is almost over," Cleopas enjoined.

The stranger complied. Cleopas marveled at the excitement, the vitality that he felt. Only this morning he had felt a deadness in his soul, and now he was alive as he had never been before.

They sat down to supper. Cleopas and Rachel turned to their guest expectantly, as they would a rabbi. He took the bread and, holding it up, gave thanks to His Father. He then broke it and gave it to them.

Suddenly they saw who He was. As if a veil had been lifted, they saw the face of their beloved Master. Just as suddenly, He vanished from their sight.

Can you imagine what it would have been like to listen to Jesus explain the Scriptures? No one could explain them as He could — He was the author!

Luke tells us that Jesus "explained to them what was said in all the Scriptures concerning Himself" (Luke 24:27). All of Scripture points to Jesus, and, ultimately, to His finished work on Calvary. From Genesis to Revelation, God reveals His plan of salvation. That salvation was accomplished when Jesus suffered and died in our place.

INTRODUCTION

Background

What better time of the year to look at God's plan of salvation than the weeks preceding Good Friday and Easter? Since the early days of the church, this has been a season of self-examination, sorrow for sin, and commitment to Christ. The six weeks before Holy Week known as Lent (Anglo-Saxon for "the lengthening of days") provides a perfect opportunity for teaching our children about Jesus' death for us.

The beginnings of Lent can be seen in the early church's practice of fasting before the Paschal feast, the celebration of Christ's death and resurrection on Easter Sunday. Easter became a time for baptizing new believers, based on the Scripture "We were therefore buried with him through baptism into death in order that, just as Christ was raised from the dead through the glory of the Father, we too may live a new life" (Romans 6:4). Fasting preceded baptism as a means of spiritual preparation.

When Constantine declared Christianity a legal religion (A.D. 313), Christianity became very popular. Persecution, which had sifted out the "nominal Christians," was no longer a threat. But now those who converted did not need to be so committed. It was at this time that Lent was lengthened to the six-week period preceding Holy Week. The purpose was to strengthen the commitment of those in the church. It also served to prepare those who would be baptized into the church on Easter.

On Easter Sunday, we, like the early Christians, celebrate our "baptism into Christ" through His death and resurrection. It seems fitting that we too prepare for this celebration by examining our walk with Christ. Are there bad habits in our lives that we need to forsake? Are there good habits, like prayer and Bible study, that we should establish? This season reminds us to look at these things. In the shadow of the Cross, Jesus calls us to reexamine our commitment to Him.

Overview

Jesus explained to Cleopas and "the other disciple" (whom I have called Rachel) that all of Scripture points to Himself, to His death and resurrection. This chapter is designed to demonstrate this. Beginning with the story of the first sin, the need for a Savior is established. God's words to the serpent contain the promise that one day a Son of man would destroy the evil one (Genesis 3:15). This victory would be bought with suffering, however. "The bruised heel" foreshadows Jesus' suffering and death on the Cross.

Next we will look at three Old Testament "types" of the death of Jesus Christ. A type is a character or event that anticipates God's later work of salvation in Christ. God was giving His people clues as to how He would someday fulfil His promises.

We will consider the near-sacrifice of Isaac as a picture of how God would provide a substitute for us (Genesis 22:1-14). The story of the first Passover (Exodus 12:1-39) paints a vivid portrait of Jesus, the Lamb of God, who would take away the sin of the world. The lifting up of the bronze serpent in the wilderness (Numbers 21:4-9) prefigures the lifting up of Jesus on the Cross.

The two weeks before Holy Week will focus on Jesus' predictions of His death and resurrection—the parable of the tenants (Matthew 21:33-46), and Jesus' anointing at Bethany (John 12:1-11).

Beginning on Palm Sunday, there is one family time for each day until Easter. During Holy Week, we will look at the events of that most important week of Jesus' life. So much happened in such a short span of time—and it was all so significant. More than one third of the entire Gospel of John is devoted to the events of that week! We will follow Matthew's more succinct account (Matthew 26-28).

Special Instructions

The family project for this season is a double banner—the first depicting the road to the Cross, and the second depicting the risen Christ. The Road to Calvary Banner can be used as a visual aid and focal point for the family times before Easter. For each family time, there is a corresponding figure that is added to the road. Then on Easter morning, the Road to Calvary Banner is covered up by the gold Easter Banner. Jesus is risen! He has conquered sin and death!

There will be one family time per week during the six weeks prior to Palm Sunday. During Holy Week (starting with Palm Sunday and ending on Easter Sunday), there is a family time for each day.

The Saturday before Easter is a time of preparation for a special family Easter celebration. Parents need to think through why it was important that Jesus be raised from the dead. The entire family will enjoy preparing for a fun "Holy Treasure Hunt."

The Holy Treasure Hunt can be used instead of or in addition to the usual Easter egg hunt. The hidden "treasures" are objects from the passages the family has been reading (e.g., a bottle of perfume to represent Jesus' anointing at Bethany). This is a fun way to review and reinforce all that the children have learned.

A time of family worship and reflection concludes the Easter celebration.

FAMILY PROJECT

The Road to Calvary Banner

Materials
- ½ yard of 36-inch-wide black felt
- ½ yard of 36-inch-wide green felt
- ½ yard of 36-inch-wide gold felt
- Green thread
- Gold thread
- Tacky glue (glue for fabrics)

- 13 adhesive-backed Velcro fasteners — black circles or one 12-inch strip regular black Velcro (to be cut and sewn on)

- 1 dowel, ⅝-inch diameter, 21 inches long

- Felt sheets (8½″ × 11″) in the following colors and quantities: grey (2), white (1), orange (1), red (1), brown (1), flesh (1), purple (1)

- 1 length of cord, ⅛-inch diameter, 36 inches long

Instructions

1. Cut the green felt in the shape of a hill with the dimensions shown in Figure 3A. (Note: save cut-away felt for later use.)

2. Sew hill to black background, using green thread. Stitch around entire perimeter of green felt (see Figure 3B).

3. Trace and cut out the patterns on pp. 251-257.

4. Cut out the felt pieces for each of the patterns cut in step 3. Colors and quantities are noted on the patterns.

5. Apply adhesive side of hook (fuzzy) Velcro fasteners to the center of the back of each grey felt circle. Or if you bought regular Velcro, cut Velcro into ¾-inch lengths. Hand sew hook (fuzzy) Velcro fasteners to the center of the back of each grey felt circle. This is more time consuming than using the adhesive-backed Velcro, but it is more durable.

6. Glue the felt figures onto the front side of the grey circles as shown on pp. 251-257. (There will be 13 circles.)

7. Apply adhesive side of loop Velcro fasteners to the green and black banner at the approximate locations shown in Figure 3C (13 total). Or, if you are using regular Velcro, sew the loop fasteners at the appropriate locations.

8. Trace and cut out the patterns on pp. 246, 248-249.

9. Cut out the felt pieces for each of the patterns cut in step 8. Note: these pieces will be used to make the figure of Jesus pictured on p. 247 and the words "HE IS RISEN."

10. Glue the felt pieces cut out in step 9 to the gold felt as shown in Figure 3D and on p. 247.

11. Draw Jesus' eyes, nose, and mouth using a fine-point black marker as shown on p. 247.

12. Sew gold banner to green/black banner along top edge using gold thread (see Figure 3E).

13. Sew a second seam 1 inch down from the first seam (see Figure 3F). This forms the casing for the dowel.

14. Drill a hole in the dowel ¾ inch from each end (see Figure 3G). If a drill is not available, use Option 2 in step 16.

15. Insert dowel into casing.

16. *Option 1*
Stiffen ends of cord by wrapping with tape. Draw ends of cord through holes at ends of dowel and knot or tie cord (see Figure 3H).

Option 2
Tie cord around ends of dowel. Glue cord to dowel so that cord will not slide toward center when hung (see Figure 3I).

Using the Road to Calvary Banner

1. Flip the Easter Banner over, in back of the Calvary Banner. Hang on wall.

2. Place grey felt circles in a manila envelope. Keep this envelope with your Bible and this book.

3. At the end of each family time, allow a child to put the appropriate circle on the banner. Start from the bottom and work your way up to the Cross, then over to the tomb.

4. On Easter Sunday, flip the Easter Banner back over the Road to Calvary.

Alternative:

If you don't have the time or inclination to make the felt banner, use posterboard and construction paper instead. Your children can color or paint the hill, cut out and glue the symbols, and the like. Then simply tape each circle to the poster as you go through your family times.

Figure 3A

green
felt
24"
28"
18"

Figure 3B

18"
black felt
green
felt
36"

Figure 3C

2" distance from top of hill to fastener
black
green
4" min. between fasteners (applies to all fasteners)
3" min. between fastener and edge of banner (applies to all fasteners)

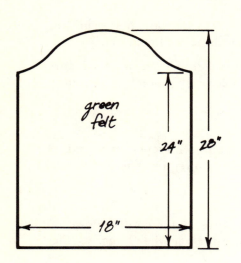

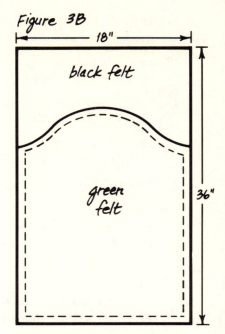

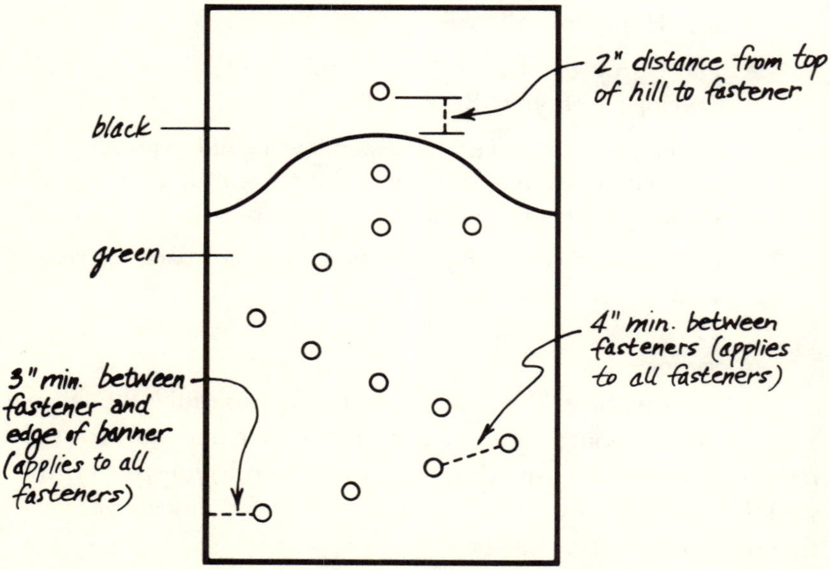

Figure 3D

Figure 3E

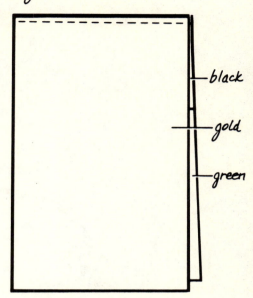

black

gold

green

Figure 3F

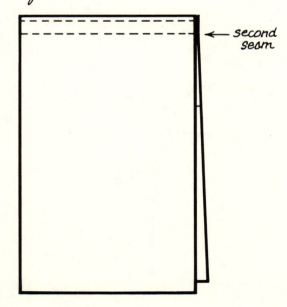

← second seam

Figure 3G

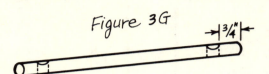

Figure 3H

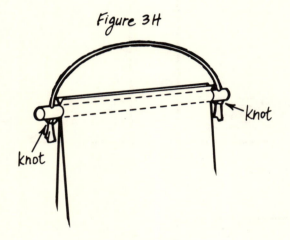

knot

knot

Figure 3I

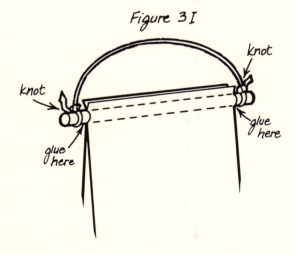

knot

knot

glue
here

glue
here

FAMILY TIMES AROUND GOD'S WORD

Week One (Seven Weeks Before Easter)

Explain:

When God created the world, He made everything good. The man and the woman (Adam and Eve) loved God and never even thought of doing anything wrong until one day . . .

Read:
Genesis 3:1-19

Discuss:

1. Adam and Eve decided that they would disobey a known command of God. That is what sin is. Ever since then, people have wanted to do things their way instead of obeying what God says to do. This has brought many problems. Can you think of sins or wrong things that you do every day? What problems do they bring?

2. Do you think that if you tried very hard, you could keep from doing anything wrong for the rest of your life? Why or why not?

3. In verse 14, God made a special promise. Can you figure out what the promise is?

Memorize:
Romans 3:23

"For all have sinned and fall short of the glory of God."

Pray:

Lord, I know that every day I do wrong things that make You unhappy. I also know that I can't be good enough to go to heaven. Thank You for sending me a Savior, just as You promised. Because of Jesus, You forgive me. Thank You, Lord. In Jesus' name. Amen.

Sing:

"Come, Ye Sinners, Poor and Needy" (*HWC* 334) or "Just As I Am" (*HWC* 342)

> Come, ye sinners, poor and needy,
> Weak and wounded, sick and sore;
> Jesus ready stands to save you,
> Full of pity, love, and pow'r.
> I will arise and go to Jesus,
> He will embrace me in His arms;
> In the arms of my dear Savior,
> O, there are ten thousand charms.

Do:

Look at the circle that has a tree on it. This is the tree of the knowledge of good and evil. It reminds us of the first sin and the need for a Savior. Place this circle at the bottom of the road to Calvary.

Week Two (Six Weeks Before Easter)

Explain:

A sacrifice was something that people gave to God — to show Him that they loved Him or that they were sorry for their sin. Usually the sacrifice was a young animal that was killed and burned on an altar as an offering to God. This passage tells us of how God gave Abraham a hard test. He asked Abraham to sacrifice something he loved more than anything in the world.

Read:
Genesis 22:1-14

Discuss:

1. Isaac was the special child that God had promised Abraham many years before. Abraham and Sarah had waited for many years for their special baby. What did God tell Abraham to do? How do you suppose Abraham felt?

2. When Isaac asked what they were going to use for a sacrifice, what did Abraham say? Was he right?

3. This happened many, many years before Jesus was born (2,000). Even then, God knew exactly what He was going to do. It was His plan to send Jesus to earth to die for our sins. This is a picture of God giving His one and only precious Son to die in our place. Why did God do this?

Memorize:
John 3:16

"For God so loved the world that he gave his one and only Son, that whoever believes in him shall not perish but have eternal life."

Pray:
Thank You, Father, for loving us so much that You sent Your precious Son, Jesus to die for us. In Jesus' name. Amen.

Sing:
"Hallelujah, What a Savior!" (*HWC* 175)

"Man of Sorrows," what a name
For the Son of God who came
Ruined sinners to reclaim!
Hallelujah! What a Savior!

Bearing shame and scoffing rude,
In my place condemned He stood;
Sealed my pardon with His blood:
Hallelujah! What a Savior!

Do:
Look at the circle with the altar and flame. This reminds us of the sacrifice that God asked Abraham to make. It also reminds us that God sacrificed His only Son for us. Place the circle on the next step up the road to Calvary.

Week Three (Five Weeks Before Easter)
Explain:
Do you remember the story of Moses and the burning bush? The bad king of Egypt, Pharaoh, was hurting the children of Israel. God told Moses to talk to Pharaoh. God wanted Pharaoh to let His people go so that they could move to the land that God

had promised them. But Pharaoh didn't want to obey God. God gave Pharaoh many chances, but still Pharaoh wouldn't listen to Him. Finally God had to take away something that Pharaoh loved very much so that he would listen. God sent an angel to kill Pharaoh's oldest son, as well as the oldest sons in all the land. But God had a special plan for the children of Israel so that their oldest sons wouldn't be killed.

Read:
Exodus 12:21-30

Discuss:
1. Why do you think this was called Passover?
2. The lamb that they killed was supposed to be a young male, "without defect" or perfect. How was that lamb like Jesus? Read what John the Baptist said of Jesus in John 1:29.
3. What saved the children of Israel from death? How did Jesus save us? What do we need to do? (Just as each Israelite family needed to put the blood on the doorposts of his home, so each person much personally receive Jesus as His Savior.)

Memorize:
Isaiah 53:6

> "We all, like sheep, have gone astray,
> each of us has turned to his own way;
> and the Lord has laid on him
> the iniquity of us all."

Pray:
Lord Jesus, we thank You that You came to die in our place so that we can live forever with You. Thank You that You are that perfect Lamb of God, who takes away the sin of the world. In Jesus' name. Amen.

Sing:
"Hallelujah, What a Savior!" (*HWC* 175) or "Worthy Is the Lamb" (*HWC* 180)

Guilty, vile, and helpless, we:
Spotless Lamb of God was He:
"Full atonement!" can it be?
Hallelujah! What a Savior!

Week Four (Four Weeks Before Easter)

Explain:

This story is about Moses and God's people, the children of Israel. God was showing them the way to the new land that He would give them. On the way, they had to cross a long desert. The people got tired and forgot about God and the new land.

Read:
Numbers 21:4-9

Discuss:

1. Why were the people dying? Could they make themselves better?

2. When Moses prayed for the people, what did the Lord tell Moses to do? How were the people saved?

3. Read John 3:14, 15. The story of Moses and the bronze serpent is another picture that God gave His people to show them what Jesus would do when He would come many years later. We are like the children of Israel. We can't save ourselves from our sin any more than they could save themselves from the poisonous snakes. God sent Jesus, who was lifted up on the Cross. If we look at Him, or trust in Him as our Savior, we will be saved. Parents, tell about when you first trusted in Jesus as your Savior.

Memorize:
Romans 6:23

"For the wages of sin is death, but the gift of God is eternal life in Christ Jesus our Lord."

Pray:
Lord, thank You that You have sent Jesus to save us from our sins. Without Him we are dying in our sins just like the chil-

dren of Israel. I trust in His work on the Cross to save me. In
Jesus' name. Amen.

Sing:

"Beneath the Cross of Jesus" (*HWC* 183) or "Hallelujah,
What a Savior!" (*HWC* 175)

> Beneath the Cross of Jesus
> I fain would take my stand—
> The shadow of a mighty Rock
> Within a weary land;
> A home within the wilderness,
> A rest upon the way,
> From the burning of the noontide heat,
> And the burden of the day.
>
> Upon that Cross of Jesus
> Mine eyes at times can see
> The very dying form of One
> Who suffered there for me;
> And from my smitten heart with tears
> Two wonders I confess—
> The wonders of redeeming love
> And my unworthiness.

Do:

Look at the circle with the snake on a pole. This is like the
snake that Moses made and lifted up for the people to look at. It
reminds us that Jesus was lifted up on a Cross so that we could
be saved.

Week Five (Three Weeks Before Easter)

Explain:

This is a parable or a story that Jesus told to teach a lesson.
Some of the people listening to Jesus were planning a way to kill
Him. Jesus knew this, and He knew that He would die. That
was the reason He came. He told this story to show them that
God sent Him and that He was God's Son.

Read:
Matthew 21:33-46

Discuss:

1. Who are some of the people in this story? What happened?

2. The landowner is supposed to be God. The farmers who are taking care of the land for Him are the Jews, God's special people. Who are the servants that God sent? Who was the Son?

3. Think about the bad men who were listening, all the while thinking about how they could kill Jesus. How do you think they felt? Did Jesus love them too?

Memorize:

Romans 5:8

"But God demonstrates his own love for us in this: While we were still sinners, Christ died for us."

Pray:

Thank You, Lord, that You knew why You came to earth. You knew that You had to die so that we could have a way to God. Thank You for loving us so much. In Jesus' name. Amen.

Sing:

"When I Survey the Wondrous Cross" (*HWC* 185)

When I survey the wondrous Cross
On which the Prince of Glory died,
My richest gain I count but loss,
And pour contempt on all my pride.

Forbid it, Lord, that I should boast,
Save in the death of Christ, my God;
All the vain things that charm me most,
I sacrifice them to His blood.

Do:

Look at the circle showing the bunch of grapes. This reminds us of the vineyard where the evil farmers killed the landowner's son. The drop of blood reminds us that Jesus bled and died for us. Place this circle on the next step of the road to Calvary.

Week Six (Two Weeks Before Easter)

Explain:

As we learned last week, Jesus knew that He was going to be killed. He came to earth for that very reason, so that He could die for our sins. When the right time had come, Jesus started heading for Jerusalem where all this would happen. The story we are about to read took place exactly one week and one day before Jesus died. Remember that Jesus knew what was going to happen to Him. How do you think He felt, as He was having dinner with some of His best friends?

Read:
John 12:1-11

Discuss:

1. Where was Jesus having dinner? What did Mary do?
2. Why do you think Mary did this?
3. Who got mad about it? Why?
4. What did Jesus say about it? Jesus knew that this perfume was like Mary's whole bank account — it was all that she had. She was saying to Jesus, "I love you so much, Jesus, that I want to give you everything, even my most precious possession." Do you think that Jesus wants us to give anything to Him? What?

Memorize:
1 Peter 3:18a

"For Christ died for sins once for all, the righteous for the unrighteous, to bring you to God."

Pray:

Jesus, You gave everything You had for me. Now I give You everything I have. Take control of my life and help me to live for You and do what makes You happy. In Jesus' name. Amen.

Sing:
"When I Survey the Wondrous Cross" (*HWC* 185)

See, from His head, His hands, His feet,
Sorrow and love flow mingled down;
Did e'er such love and sorrow meet,
Or thorns compose so rich a crown?

Were the whole realm of nature mine,
That were a present far too small;
Love so amazing, so divine,
Demands my soul, my life, my all.

Do:

Look at the circle with the bottle of perfume on it. This reminds us that Mary gave her very best thing to Jesus. Place this circle on the next step of the road to Calvary.

Palm Sunday

Explain:

The Jewish people had been waiting for hundreds of years for the Messiah, the special person sent by God to save them. They thought that this person would become a great king who would make their country important and rich again. The Bible told them that this King would come into Jerusalem riding on a donkey.

Read:
Matthew 21:1-11

Discuss:

1. Why were the people so excited when they saw Jesus that day?

2. Jesus was that special King, but He came, not to make them important and rich, but to save them from sin. What about Jesus makes you excited?

3. Today Jesus is the King of heaven and earth. But He also wants to be the King of our lives. What does this mean? How can Jesus be your King?

Memorize:
John 11:25-26a

"Jesus said to her, 'I am the resurrection and the life. He who believes in me will live, even though he dies; and whoever lives and believes in me will never die.'"

Pray:

Lord, we're excited that You are the King of heaven. Help us to serve and obey You as our King. In Jesus' name. Amen.

Sing:

"Crown Him with Many Crowns" (*HWC* 234) or "All Glory, Laud, and Honor" (*HWC* 173)

> Crown Him with many crowns,
> The Lamb upon His throne;
> Hark! how the heav'nly anthem drowns
> All music but its own.
> Awake, my soul, and sing
> Of Him who died for thee,
> And hail Him as thy matchless King
> Thru all eternity.

Do:

Look at the circle which shows a palm branch. The people laid palm branches in the street to welcome Jesus as their King. Place this circle on the next step on the road to Calvary.

Monday of Holy Week

Explain:

Today we will be reading about the Last Supper. This meal that Jesus shared with His disciples is called the Last Supper because it was the last meal that Jesus ate with His friends before He died. This was a very special meal, probably the most important celebration in Jesus' life.

Read:
Matthew 26:14-30

Discuss:

1. What were Jesus and the disciples celebrating? Does any-

one remember what the Passover was about? (Read Exodus 12:1-30 or summarize.)

2. Breaking the unleavened bread (crackers) and drinking the wine were a very important part of this celebration. What new meaning did Jesus give to these things?

3. Jesus knew which one of His disciples had become His enemy. He also knew that soon He would be dying, and His friends would all run away instead of staying with Him. And He knew how very hard it would be to die on the Cross for the sins of the whole world. How do you think Jesus and His disciples were feeling?

Memorize:

1 John 4:10

"This is love: not that we loved God, but that he loved us and sent his Son as an atoning sacrifice for our sins."

Pray:

Thank You, Lord Jesus, that Your body was broken and Your blood was shed for us. In Jesus' name. Amen.

Sing:

"I Lay My Sins on Jesus" (*HWC* 340)

I lay my sins on Jesus,
The spotless Lamb of God;
He bears them all, and frees us
From the accursed load.
I bring my guilt to Jesus,
To wash my crimson stains
White in His Blood most precious
Till not a spot remains.

Do:

Look at the circle which shows the loaf of bread and the cup of wine. This reminds us of Jesus' Last Supper with His friends. It also reminds us that soon He would die for our sins. Place this circle on the next step on the Road to Calvary banner.

Tuesday of Holy Week

Explain:

After the Passover meal, Jesus and His disciples went to a
garden where Jesus often went to pray. This was a place called
Gethsemane, on the Mount of Olives, just outside Jerusalem.

Read:

Matthew 26:31-46

Discuss:

1. What did Jesus go to Gethsemane to do? Why?

2. What were the disciples doing while Jesus was praying?
How do you think that made Jesus feel?

3. Why is it so important to pray when we are very worried
or upset about something?

Review:

1 John 4:10

"This is love; not that we loved him but that he loved us, and
sent his Son as an atoning sacrifice for our sins."

Pray:

Lord, so often we're like the disciples — we fall asleep instead
of praying. Or we are just too busy for You. Help us to pray
when we are upset or worried. Help us to give our problems to
You. In Jesus' name. Amen.

Sing:

"Jesus Paid It All" (*HWC* 210)

> I hear the Savior say,
> "Thy strength indeed is small!
> Child of weakness, watch and pray
> Find in Me thine all in all."
> Jesus paid it all,
> All to Him I owe;
> Sin had left a crimson stain —
> He washed it white as snow.

Do:

Look at the circle that shows a praying hand. Jesus went to the garden of Gethsemane to talk to His Father. Place this circle on the next step on the road to Calvary.

Wednesday of Holy Week

Explain:

As Jesus was talking to His disciples in the garden, suddenly His enemies arrived. They were led by Judas, Jesus' disciple who became His enemy. They came to take Him away. The Jewish leaders wanted Jesus dead, but they didn't want to kill Him themselves because that was against God's Law. So instead, they got people to lie about Jesus so that the ruler, Pilate, would have Jesus killed. Of course, that was just as bad as killing Him themselves, but they were so evil that they didn't really know what makes God happy or unhappy.

Read:

Matthew 26:47-75

Discuss:

1. What did Jesus do when the Jewish leaders came to arrest Him? Why didn't He fight or call down angels to help Him?

2. How did the Jewish leaders treat Jesus?

3. Where did the disciples go? Why did Peter say that he didn't know Jesus?

Review:

Romans 5:8

"But God demonstrates his own love for us in this: While we were still sinners, Christ died for us."

Pray:

Lord Jesus, help me not to be afraid to tell other people that I know You. In Jesus' name. Amen.

Sing:

"Rock of Ages" (*HWC* 204)

Rock of Ages, cleft for me,
Let me hide myself in Thee
Let the water and the blood,
From Thy riven side which flowed,
Be of sin the double cure,
Cleanse me from its guilt and pow'r.

Nothing in my hand I bring,
Simply to Thy Cross I cling
Naked, come to Thee for dress,
Helpless, look to Thee for grace.
Foul, I to the fountain fly,
Wash me, Savior, or I die!

Do:

Look at the circle that shows a rooster. This is like the bird that crowed right after Peter said that he didn't know Jesus. Place this circle on the next step on the road to Calvary.

Maundy Thursday

Explain:

Today is called "Maundy Thursday." The word *Maundy* comes from the Latin word for *mandate* or *command*. On this night, Jesus gave His disciples a new commandment—to love one another. This was the actual night He celebrated the Passover that we read about on Monday. When He broke the bread and gave them the cup to drink, He gave them another command. Do you remember what it was?

Read:
Matthew 27:11-31

Discuss:

1. Pilate was the Roman governor who ruled over the Jews. It was against the Law for the Jewish leaders who hated Jesus to kill Him. They had to get Pilate to give an order that Jesus be killed. How did they do this?

2. When the Jewish leaders were telling Pilate lies about Jesus, what did Jesus say? Why not?

3. Why did Pilate give the order for Jesus to be killed? Did washing his hands make him innocent of killing Jesus?

Review:
Isaiah 53:6

"We all, like sheep, have gone astray, each of us has turned to his own way; and the Lord has laid on him the iniquity of us all."

John 3:16

"For God so loved the world that he gave his one and only Son, that whoever believes in him shall not perish but have eternal life."

Pray:
Lord, when the time comes that everyone wants me to do something that is wrong, help me to say no. Help me to be strong enough to stand up for what is right. In Jesus' name. Amen.

Sing:
"O Sacred Head, Now Wounded" (*HWC* 178)

O sacred Head, now wounded,
With grief and shame weighed down,
Now scornfully surrounded
With thorns Thy only crown:
How pale Thou art with anguish,
With sore abuse and scorn,
How does that visage languish,
Which once was bright as morn!

What Thou, my Lord, hast suffered
Was all for sinners' gain;
Mine, mine was the transgression,
But Thine the deadly pain.
Lo, here I fall, my Savior;
'Tis I deserve Thy place;
Look on me with Thy favor,
Assist me with Thy grace.

What language shall I borrow
To thank Thee, dearest friend,
For this Thy dying sorrow,
Thy pity without end?
O make me Thine forever,
And should I fainting be,
Lord let me never never
Outlive my love to Thee.

Do:

Look at the circle that shows a crown of thorns. The soldiers made fun of Jesus and hurt Him by putting this on His head. Place this circle on the next step on the road to Calvary.

Good Friday

Explain:

Today we remember Jesus' death on the cross. We call it Good Friday. It seems a strange name for such a sad day. Can you think of a reason why Jesus' death is good? If you can't right now, perhaps by the end of this family time, you will know the answer.

Read:
Matthew 27:32-56

Discuss:

1. What did people say about Jesus as He was hanging on the cross?

2. What did Jesus cry out from the cross (v. 46)? The greatest pain that Jesus felt was not from hanging on the cross. It was the pain of being separated from God the Father. Jesus was carrying all our sin on Him as He hung on the Cross (see 2 Corinthians 5:21). Because God cannot even look on sin He had to turn His face from Jesus.

3. What amazing thing happened the moment that Jesus died? The curtain of the temple separated the Holy of Holies — a special room that was reserved for God — from the rest of the temple where the people were. By tearing the curtain, God was showing us that He had made a way for us to come to Him.

Pray:

Thank you so much, Lord Jesus, for dying for my sin so that I could come to God and know Him, now and forever. In Jesus' name. Amen.

Review:

1 Peter 3:18(a)

"For Christ died for sin once for all, the righteous for the unrighteous, to bring us to God."

Sing:

"The Old Rugged Cross" (*HWC* 186) or "At the Cross" ("Alas! And Did My Savior Bleed?") (*HWC* 188)

> Alas! and did my Savior bleed?
> And did my Sov'reign die?
> Would He devote that sacred head
> For sinners such as I!
>
> Was it for crimes that I have done
> He groaned upon the tree?
> Amazing pity! grace unknown!
> And love beyond degree!
>
> Well might the sun in darkness hide
> And shut His glories in,
> When Christ, the mighty Maker, died
> For man the creature's sin.

Do:

Look at the circle that shows the Cross. Place this circle on the top of the hill of Calvary.

Saturday of Holy Week

Read:

Matthew 27:57-66

Discuss:

1. What happened to Jesus' body? Read Isaiah 53:9. Hundreds of years before Jesus was born, the prophet told that God's

Son would die with criminals and have a rich man's tomb. God had it all planned out from the very beginning.

2. Who was watching?

3. Why did the Jewish leaders ask for the tomb to be guarded?

Review:

John 11:25-26a

"Jesus said to her, 'I am the resurrection and the life. He who believes in me will live, even though he died; and whoever lives and believes in me will never die.'"

Pray:

Thank You, Lord, that all this happened according to Your plan. Thank You for what You did on the Cross so that I can be free from guilt and sin. In Jesus' name. Amen.

Sing:

"Were You There?" (*HWC* 181)

> Were you there when they crucified my Lord?
> Were you there when they crucified my Lord?
> O! Sometimes it causes me to tremble, tremble, tremble!
> Were you there when they crucified my Lord?

> Were you there when they nailed Him to the tree?
> (etc.)

> Were you there when they laid Him in the tomb?
> (etc.)

Do:

Look at the circle that shows a cave. Jesus' tomb was probably a cave in a rocky hill. Place this circle on the last Velcro fastener on the road to Calvary. It should be down the hill from the Cross.

Also, prepare for your Resurrection Day celebration.

Preparing for Resurrection Day:

1. Decide which of the Gospel accounts you will use tomorrow as you act out the events of the Resurrection:

Matthew 28:1-10

Mark 16:1-20

Luke 24:1-49

John 20:1-31

2. Assemble any costumes or props for acting out the stories.

3. Collect and/or make the items that will be hidden for the Holy Treasure Hunt. Be sure to include the children in the preparations. The preparations are half the fun, plus they heighten the excitement for the coming event.

4. Prepare to discuss the significance of the Resurrection. What do the following passages teach about this question:

"Why was it important that Jesus be raised from the dead?"

Acts 2:22-32

Romans 6:5-11

1 Corinthians 15:12-22

Ephesians 1:19-23

FAMILY CELEBRATION

Easter morning reveals that the dark road to Calvary has been covered up by the bright gold banner. The Easter banner proclaims that "He Is Risen!"

The Christian tradition for Easter morning is to worship the risen Lord. This worship service is the climax of the entire church year. Going to church should be the highest priority for Easter Sunday.

In addition to this, perhaps after the Easter dinner, a family worship time is appropriate. This section includes a brief format for family worship on Easter.

Also included is a fun family activity to reinforce the events of the Easter season. This activity, called the "Holy Treasure Hunt," can either replace or accompany an Easter egg hunt.

Family Worship on Easter

Leader:
The Lord is risen!

All:
He is risen, indeed!

Sing:
"Christ the Lord Is Risen Today" (*HWC* 217)

> Christ the Lord is ris'n today, Alleluia!
> Sons of men and angels say: Alleluia!
> Raise your joys and triumphs high, Alleluia!
> Sing, ye heav'ns, and earth reply: Alleluia!
>
> Lives again our glorious King, Alleluia!
> Where, O death, is now thy sting? Alleluia!
> Dying once He all doth save, Alleluia!
> Where thy victory, O grave? Alleluia!
>
> Love's redeeming work is done, Alleluia!
> Fought the fight, the battle won, Alleluia!
> Death in vain forbids Him rise, Alleluia!
> Christ has opened Paradise, Alleluia!
>
> Soar we now where Christ has led, Alleluia!
> Foll'wing our exalted Head, Alleluia!
> Made like Him, like Him we rise, Alleluia!
> Ours the cross, the grave, the skies, Alleluia!

Act Out:
Select one of the following Gospel accounts of the Resurrection to act out. Props and costumes are not necessary but may be lots of fun. Read the passage(s) over and try to faithfully perform the events as recorded in the Gospels.

> Matthew 28:1-10
> Mark 16:1-20
> Luke 24:1-49
> John 20:1-31

Discuss:

Why was it important that Jesus be raised from the dead?

To answer this question, look up the following passages:

Acts 2:22-32

Romans 6:5-11

1 Corinthians 15:12-22

Ephesians 1:19-23

Pray:

We praise You, O Christ, for the great power that You had to break the chains of death. Thank You that right now we can have new life in You, and someday we will have new bodies that will never die. In Jesus' name. Amen.

Sing:

"Crown Him with Many Crowns" (*HWC* 234)

Crown Him with many crowns,
The Lamb upon His throne;
Hark! how the heav'nly anthem drowns
All music but its own.
Awake, my soul, and sing
Of Him who died for thee,
And hail Him as thy matchless King
Through all eternity.

Crown Him the Lord of life,
Who triumphed o'er the grave,
And rose victorious in the strife
For those He came to save;
His glories now we sing,
Who died and rose on high,
Who died eternal life to bring,
And lives, that death may die.

Crown Him the Lord of love;
Behold His hands and side,
Those wounds yet visible above,
In beauty glorified:
All hail, Redeemer, hail!
For Thou hast died for me:
Thy praise and glory shall not fail
Throughout eternity.

Holy Treasure Hunt

Preparation:

Involve the children in collecting and making the items to be used. Some are ordinary household items (bottle of perfume, sponge), others will have to be made of paper, wood, or whatever materials you have on hand.

When the children are in bed or are out of the way, hide the items.

Items:

1. Thirty silver coins (Matthew 26:15). Use nickels. These may be hidden separately or together in a bag.
2. Bottle of perfume (John 12:3)
3. Clean white rag in strips (Matthew 27:59)
4. Cross (Matthew 27:32-35)
5. Sponge (Matthew 27:48)
6. Dice (Matthew 27:35)
7. Crackers (Matthew 26:26) (Suggestion: put in plastic bag)
8. Cup (Matthew 26:27, 39, 42)
9. Palm (Matthew 21:8)
10. Thorny branch (Matthew 27:29)

Add to this list any items that you think of.

To Play:

1. Have the children go on a hunt to find the items. Because they were involved in the preparation, they know exactly what they are looking for, but it might be a good idea to give them a list.

2. When all the items have been located and gathered up, come back together and have the children show what they have found.

3. As each item is displayed, ask the children what part that item played in the events of Holy Week ("Do you remember a sponge in anything we read this week?").

4. If your children can read and are stumped on any of the items, give them the Bible reference as a clue. Let them look it up in the Bible and figure it out.

Come down, O love divine,
Seek thou this soul of mine,
And visit it with thine own ardor glowing.
O Comforter, draw near,
Within my heart appear,
And kindle it, thy holy flame bestowing.

O let it freely burn,
Till earthly passions turn
To dust and ashes in its heat consuming;
And let thy glorious light
Shine ever on my sight,
And clothe me round, the while my path illuming.

Bianco da Siena, 1434

FOUR

GOD'S SPECIAL GIFT

Pentecost

"What's the Holy Ghost, Mom?" asked Andrew as his mother tucked the covers around him.

"That's a big question for this late hour," she smiled. "Where did you hear about the Holy Ghost?"

"In church on Sunday, we sang 'Glory to the Father, and to the Son, and to the Holy Ghost.'"

"Yes, that's right, we did," Mom replied as she sat down on the edge of the bed. "Holy Ghost is another name for the Holy Spirit. Do you know about the Holy Spirit?"

"Sort of," Andrew said. "Is He one of God's angels?"

"The Holy Spirit is God, just as the Father and Jesus are God," Mom explained. "But unlike Jesus, the Holy Spirit is invisible. Remember when you asked Jesus to be your Lord and Savior? Well, it was the Holy Spirit, or the invisible Spirit of God, who came to live within you then. Does that make sense?"

"I think so," Andrew said.

"Hmm. Let me see if I can make it a little simpler," Mom puzzled. "I know. Jesus was trying to explain it to Nicodemus, and He compared the Holy Spirit to the wind. You can't see the wind, but you can see that it is blowing by the way that the trees are bending and rocking."

"I get it!" interrupted Andrew. "You can't see the Holy Spirit, but you can see what He does!"

"Exactly," said Mom. "The Holy Spirit makes changes in people—in us. He changes the way we think and talk and act so that we become more like Jesus."

"That's really neat!" exclaimed Andrew.

"Time for bed, honey. Maybe we should explore this together as a family," Mom suggested as she planted a kiss on Andrew's cheek.

INTRODUCTION

Background

Children harbor many confused ideas about the Holy Spirit. For that matter, so do many adults. The Holy Spirit is the most mysterious person of the Trinity. There is the tendency to either ignore Him altogether, or to magnify Him to the exclusion of the Father and the Son.

The Bible is not silent about the Holy Spirit. While it doesn't tell us everything we might want to know on this subject, Scripture does teach us some basic truths about the third person of the Trinity.

The post-Easter season is an especially appropriate time to focus on the person and work of the Holy Spirit. Jesus' last teachings included many promises concerning the One whom He would send when He went to the Father (John 14-17).

Forty days after the resurrection, Jesus ascended into heaven, just as He had said. His last words to His disciples were, "But you will receive power when the Holy Spirit comes on you; and you will be my witnesses in Jerusalem, and in all Judea and Samaria, and to the ends of the earth" (Acts 1:8).

Ten days later it happened. The disciples were gathered together (perhaps in the temple), observing the Feast of the Harvest, or Pentecost. The Holy Spirit descended upon them with both visible (tongues of fire) and audible signs (the sound of a violent wind).

From that moment on, the disciples' lives were radically and irrevocably changed. Fearful fishermen were transformed into bold and articulate ambassadors of Christ. Everywhere they went, other people's lives were touched and transformed as a result. The book of Acts is a history of the awesome working of the Holy Spirit in the fledgling church.

Overview

This chapter contains a four-week exploration of the Holy Spirit, beginning three weeks before Pentecost (four weeks after Easter) and culminating on the Day of Pentecost (seven weeks after Easter). There is one family time for each week leading up to Pentecost, then a final family worship celebration on the Day of Pentecost itself.

The first family time concerns the work of the Holy Spirit in inspiring Scripture. The second looks at His work in the body of Christ as He equips us with special gifts. The third family time relates to the fruit of the Spirit. Finally, on Pentecost Sunday, the family celebrates the giving of the Holy Spirit ten days after the Lord's ascension.

Specific Instructions

In order to reinforce the Biblical teaching on the Holy Spirit, the family project displays symbols of the various roles of the Holy Spirit. These are suspended from a mobile, which is easy for the entire family to assemble. The mobile itself illustrates Jesus' words about the Holy Spirit. It shows the movement of the invisible air currents around it, just as our lives show the working of the invisible, yet very real, Holy Spirit.

This project is designed to initiate this season. At the conclusion of each family time, a symbol related to the passage is added to the mobile. For that reason, it is best to construct the mobile first.

The mobile is not essential to the family times, however. Feel free to use, not use, or modify these ideas to suit the needs of your family.

One hymn, "Spirit of God, Descend Upon My Heart," is focused on during the family times. A different verse is given for each family time. For families with small children, this repetition will help them learn one hymn well. An alternative hymn is also listed. If your family has several favorite praise choruses about the Holy Spirit, feel free to use these instead.

FAMILY PROJECT

The family project for the season of Pentecost is a mobile representing the person and work of the Holy Spirit. The movement of the mobile as it gently twirls and sways with the air currents reminds us of the work of the Holy Spirit in our lives. Although we cannot see the Holy Spirit, just as we cannot see the air currents, we can see the effects of His work in our lives.

The mobile consists of a metal ring (made from a coat hanger) suspended horizontally from the ceiling by four strings. These strings are wrapped in red and white crepe paper streamers. The white streamers represent the Holy Spirit in the form of a dove that descended on Christ when He was baptized. The red color symbolizes the tongues of fire present above each of the disciples on the day of Pentecost. After each family time, one figure representing a particular role of the Holy Spirit is added to the mobile.

This inexpensive project can involve the entire family. Dad can bend the coat hanger, while Mom and the youngest child can tie the strings. (Mom needs an extra finger to help her tie the knots tightly.) Meanwhile, the other children can be measuring lengths of string, tracing circles, and cutting.

The Holy Spirit Mobile

Materials

- One metal coat hanger
- Kite string or yarn
- One 8 ½ inches × 11 inches sheet of heavy-weight paper, such as posterboard, tagboard, or a manila file folder
- Red and white crepe paper streamers
- Three sheets of plain white typing paper
- Scissors
- Pliers
- Crayons or markers

- Pencil
- Soup can
- Ruler
- Glue

Instructions

1. Straighten out the metal coat hanger. Then, using a pliers, make a hook on each end of the hanger (see Figure 4A).

2. Hook the two ends together so that the hanger is in the shape of a circle or ring (see Figure 4B). Wrap the metal ring with a red or white crepe paper streamer.

3. Decide where you will hang your Holy Spirit mobile. Figure out how low you want it to hang down. Measure the distance to the ceiling or fixture from which it will hang.

4. Add five inches to the measurement from Step 3. Cut four pieces of string or yarn this length.

5. Tie one end of each string onto the metal ring. Tie them in the 12 o'clock, 3 o'clock, 6 o'clock, and 9 o'clock positions (see Figure 4C).

6. Tie the other ends of the strings together in one knot over the center of the ring so that the ring will hang horizontally. (We will call these the hanger-strings.) Make sure that there is enough free string on the end so that you can tie this central knot to the plant hanger or fixture from which you will be hanging your mobile (see Figure 4D).

7. Hang up your Holy Spirit mobile. You can tie it to a light fixture, planter hook, or other high place. Or you can affix it to the ceiling with a tack or pushpin.

8. Tape one end of a crepe-paper streamer to the top of the mobile (where the four hanger-strings are knotted at the top). Loosely wrap one of the four hanger-strings by twisting the crepe paper around and around the length of the string as shown in Figure 4E. Let the other end of the crepe paper streamer dangle below the metal ring.

9. Repeat Step 8 for the other three hanger strings.

10. Trace around the bottom of a soup can on the sheet of heavy-weight paper to make five circles. Cut out these circles (see Figure 4F).

11. Use a sharp pencil to poke one hole in each circle, ¼ inch from the edge.

12. Cut four pieces of string of varying lengths. Threading it through the poked hole, tie one string to each circle (see Figure 4G). These circles will have symbols or pictures glued to them and then will be hung from the metal ring, one by one during the weeks preceding Pentecost.

Using the Holy Spirit Mobile

1. During the Pentecost family times, you will need:
   - Bible
   - *Family Celebrations*
   - Manila circles with strings attached, constructed in steps 10-12 above
   - Crayons or markers
   - Pencil
   - White typing paper
   - Scissors
   - Glue

   (You may want to keep these things together in a shoe box in a handy place so that you don't have to assemble these items each week.)

2. Each family time will focus on one particular role of the Holy Spirit. For each of these roles, there is a symbol pictured within a circle on pp. 258-259.

3. After each family time, make two tracings on plain white paper of the appropriate symbol and circle. (Specific instructions are given in the "DO" section of each family time.)

4. Color and cut out these two circles.

5. Glue these two circles to either side of one of the manila circles.

6. Tie this circle to the Holy Spirit mobile. Because there are four circles in all, you can tie one between each of the hanger-strings. The completed mobile is pictured in Figure 4H.

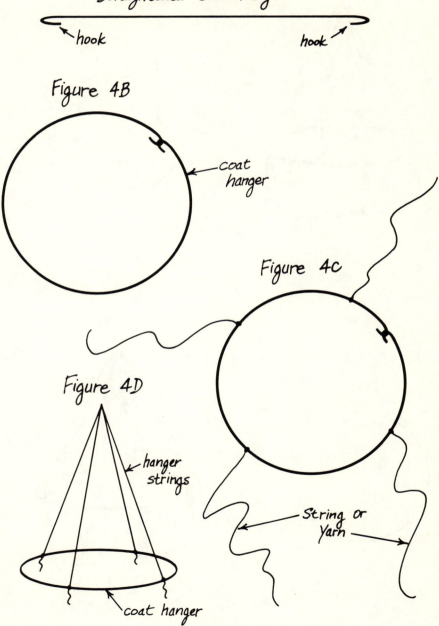

Figure 4A
Straightened Coat Hanger
hook   hook

Figure 4B
coat hanger

Figure 4C

Figure 4D
hanger strings
coat hanger
String or Yarn

Figure 4E

crepe paper

Figure 4F

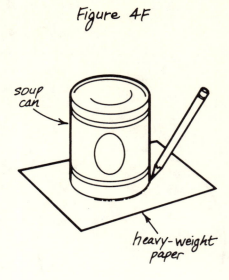

soup can

heavy-weight paper

Figure 4G

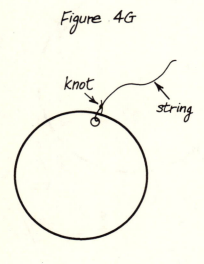

knot

string

Figure 4H

FAMILY TIMES AROUND GOD'S WORD

**Three Weeks
Before Pentecost**

The Spirit of Truth

Explain:

During Jesus' last days before His death and resurrection, He was filled with concern for His disciples. He knew that after His resurrection, He would not be with them very long. How they would miss Him after being with Him every day for three years!

He tried to explain to them about His coming death, but the disciples didn't understand. They knew enough, however, to be very sad at what Jesus was saying.

Then Jesus told them about something wonderful that would happen after He was gone. He told them that He would send them a Helper so that they would not be left alone.

This Helper was the Holy Spirit, who is the invisible Spirit of Jesus. Jesus was saying, "I have to go to heaven. But I will send my Spirit to live inside you and help you with many things."

Let's read about how the Holy Spirit would help them (and us). These are Jesus' words to His disciples.

Read:

John 14:25-26 and 16:13

Discuss:

1. What did Jesus say that the Holy Spirit would do?

2. Why is that important?

3. Several of the disciples wrote parts of the Bible in later years (Peter and Matthew). Here Jesus was promising them that the Holy Spirit would help them so that everything they wrote down about Jesus was true. The Holy Spirit led them so that what they wrote was exactly as God wanted it written. How does that make the Bible special?

4. Jesus' promise that the Holy Spirit would guide them into all truth is a promise for us as well. The Holy Spirit works through the Bible to teach us and make us more like Jesus. What do we have to do to cooperate with the Holy Spirit?

Memorize:
John 16:13(a)

"But when he, the Spirit of truth, comes, he will guide you into all truth."

Pray:
Dear Lord, thank You for giving us Your Holy Spirit so that we are never alone. Thank You that we can know that the Bible is true. And thank You that as we read it, we will learn the truth and will become more like Jesus. In Jesus' name we pray. Amen.

Sing:
"Spirit of God, Descend Upon My Heart" (*HWC* 249) or "Holy Ghost, with Light Divine" (*HWC* 248)

> Spirit of God, descend upon my heart;
> Wean it from earth, through all its pulses move;
> Stoop to my weakness, mighty as Thou art,
> And make me love Thee as I ought to love.

Do:
Trace and cut out two copies of the circle on p. 258 picturing the open Bible. Using markers or crayons, color these circles. Glue one to each side of one of the four tagboard circles on your Holy Spirit mobile.

Two Weeks Before Pentecost
Spirit of Cooperation
Explain:
Have you ever been given a job to do, but no tools with which to do it? Suppose your parents gave you the job of planting a garden, but they didn't give you a rake or a hoe or a spade? It would be impossible for you to get the soil ready for the seeds without any tools!

When Jesus left this earth, He gave His disciples a job to do. (See Matthew 28:19-20.) He commanded them, and all Christians, to go out to all parts of the world and teach people to love and obey Him. This is a very big job, but Jesus promised to be with them. It is in the Holy Spirit that Jesus was with them and is with us.

The Holy Spirit gives us all the tools we need to do the job that Jesus wants us to do. Each of us is given a different tool, or gift. The job is done as we cooperate and work together, each using the tools that the Spirit has given us.

Read:
1 Corinthians 12:4-20

Discuss:
1. The Bible tells us that God's family on earth (all Christians) is like a body. Why are we like a body?

2. Who gives us these spiritual gifts and why?

3. Spiritual gifts are not the same as talents. Playing the piano or being athletic are wonderful talents, but they are not spiritual gifts. They are abilities that you are born with. Spiritual gifts are special abilities that are given to you when you receive Jesus as your Savior and are born into God's family. Some examples are listed in verses 8-10. Go around the circle of your family, having the other family members tell each person what they think his spiritual gift is.

4. What were the eye and the foot saying in this passage? How were they feeling? Are there some parts that are more important than others? Why or why not (vv. 18-20)?

5. Talk about how each of your gifts is helpful to the other members of your family.

Memorize:
Ephesians 4:4

"There is one body and one Spirit—just as you were called to one hope when you were called."

Pray:
Thank You, heavenly Father, for sending Your Spirit to give us special gifts. We want to use our gifts to help our family, our church, and all Christians. Show us what our gifts are and how we can use them to please You and help others. In Jesus' name. Amen.

Sing:

"Spirit of God, Descend Upon My Heart" (*HWC* 249) or "Sweet, Sweet Spirit" (*HWC* 252)

> I ask no dream, no prophet ecstasies,
> No sudden rending of the veil of clay,
> No angel visitant, no opening skies;
> But take the dimness of my soul away.

Do:

Trace and cut out two copies of the circle on p. 258 picturing the body of a man. Using markers or crayons, color these circles. Glue one to each side of one of the four tagboard circles on your Holy Spirit mobile.

One Week Before Pentecost

Spirit of Christ-Likeness

Explain:

Did you make any New Year's resolutions on January 1 this year? Have you kept your resolutions? It is easy to make resolutions, but it is very difficult to keep them, to make real changes in our lives. So often we resolve never to do a certain sin or bad habit again. And before we know it, we've gone ahead and done it again! Do you think Jesus had that problem? Why not?

God has given us an answer to this problem. He gave us His Spirit to live within us, changing us from the inside out. The Holy Spirit works to help us do what is right. He is working, day-by-day, to make us more like Jesus. Let's read about the good things that He produces in our lives.

Read:

Galatians 5:22-25

Discuss:

1. The Holy Spirit takes the garbage of our lives (our sin) and throws it out. Then, in its place, He puts good, delicious

fruit. Perhaps we can best understand what this fruit is by figuring out what bad things it replaces. What is the opposite of each of the characteristics listed in verse 22?

2. Remember, this is not something that we do. It is the work of the Holy Spirit who is called alongside to help us. What are we supposed to be doing in the meantime (read verse 25 again)?

3. Can you think of someone whose life shows the fruit of the Holy Spirit? That person probably spends time with God in prayer and in Bible study. As we love God, spend special time with Him, and obey what He tells us to do in His Word, we make room in our hearts for His Spirit to do His work.

Memorize:
Galatians 5:22-23

"But the fruit of the Spirit is love, joy, peace, patience, kindness, goodness, faithfulness, gentleness and self-control. Against such things there is no law."

Pray:
Dear Lord, we want You to take away the garbage in our lives and make us more and more like You. Help us to love You and obey You, so that Your Holy Spirit is free to produce this fruit in our lives. In Jesus' name. Amen.

Sing:
"Spirit of God, Descend Upon My Heart" (*HWC* 249) or "Spirit of the Living God" (*HWC* 247)

> Hast Thou not bid me love Thee, God and King;
> All, all Thine own, soul, heart
>   and strength and mind?
> I see Thy Cross; there teach my heart to cling;
> O let me seek Thee, and O let me find!

Do:
Trace and cut out two copies of the circle on p. 259 picturing the bunch of grapes (for the fruit of the Spirit). Using markers or crayons, color these circles. Glue one to each side of one of the four tagboard circles on your Holy Spirit mobile.

FAMILY CELEBRATION

The family celebration on the day of Pentecost is comprised of two parts: a family worship time and a family fun time. The family worship time focuses on the sending of the Holy Spirit on the Day of Pentecost. The family fun time is a game aimed at reinforcing the fruit of the Holy Spirit.

Family Worship on Pentecost

Light a candle (preferably red, the color of the tongues of fire on the Day of Pentecost).

Call to Worship:

Leader:

The Lord God spoke to His prophet Joel, saying:

> "And afterward,
> I will pour out my Spirit on all people.
> Your sons and daughters will prophesy,
> your old men will dream dreams,
> your young men will see visions.
> Even on my servants, both men and women,
> I will pour out my Spirit in those days" (Joel 2:28-29).

Pray:

Leader 1:

We praise You, Lord, that You are the Spirit of Truth. You gave us Your Word, the Bible, as men of old were moved by Your Holy Spirit. Help us to read it, understand it, and obey it. Lord, in Your mercy.

All:

Hear our prayer.

Leader 2:

We praise You, Lord, that Your Spirit has made all Christians one body and has equipped us with different gifts. Help us to use our gifts to help Your family and to give You glory and honor. Lord, in Your mercy.

All:
Hear our prayer.

Leader 3:
We praise You, Lord, that Your Spirit works within us to make us like You. Help us to stay away from sin and to cooperate with Your Spirit by loving and obeying You. Lord, in Your mercy.

All:
Hear our prayer.

Leader 4:
We praise You, Lord, that You have made Your power available to us in Your Holy Spirit. Help us to use that power to be who You want us to be and do what You want us to do. Lord, in Your mercy.

All:
Hear our prayer.

Read:
Acts 1:7-11

Sing:
"Breathe on Me, Breath of God" (*HWC* 259)

> Breathe on me, Breath of God,
> Fill me with life anew,
> That I may love what Thou dost love,
> And do what Thou wouldst do.
>
> Breathe on me, Breath of God,
> Until my heart is pure,
> Until my will is one with Thine,
> To do and to endure.

Breathe on me, Breath of God,
Till I am wholly Thine,
Until this earthly part of me
Glows with Thy fire divine.

Breathe on me, Breath of God,
So shall I never die,
But live with Thee the perfect life
Of Thine Eternity.

Read:
Acts 2:1-13

Discuss:

1. What did Jesus promise His disciples before He went up into heaven?

2. The Day of Pentecost was a Jewish festival similar to our Thanksgiving. It came at the end of their barley harvest, so they gathered to give thanks to God for providing their grain and their food. In addition, they also celebrated the giving of the Law to Moses on Mount Sinai. Jews and other people who believed in God gathered in Jerusalem for this festival. They came from many parts of the world to worship God in the temple. That is probably where the disciples were as well.

3. What amazing thing happened that day? What did people see and hear?

4. From that moment on, the disciples were never the same. The Holy Spirit gave them the power to say and do things that they never could have before. (Read the book of Acts as a family to find out what the Holy Spirit did in their lives and in the world.) How has the Holy Spirit made a difference in your life? How have you changed as a result of God's work in you?

Pray:
Leader:
Gracious Father, we thank You for the gift of Your Holy Spirit. Fill us and empower us with Your Spirit that we may do Your will to the glory of Your name.

All:
Amen.

Sing:

"Spirit of God, Descend Upon My Heart" (*HWC* 249)

Spirit of God, descend upon my heart;
Wean it from earth, through all its pulses move;
Stoop to my weakness, mighty as thou art,
And make me love thee as I ought to love.

Teach me to love thee as thine angels love,
One holy passion filling all my frame:
The baptism of the heaven-descended Dove,
My heart an altar, and thy love the flame.

Extinguish the flame on the candle, explaining that God's love continues to burn in our hearts through the Holy Spirit.

Do:

Trace and cut out two copies of the circle on p. 259 picturing the flame. Using markers or crayons, color these circles. Glue one to each side of one of the four tagboard circles on your Holy Spirit mobile.

Family Fun
Holy Spirit Fruit Basket
Number of Players:
4-20

Length of Time:
10-20 minutes

Materials:
A basket or bowl for each player, pencils, as many slips of paper for each player as there are players, less one (e.g., for 5 family members, each player has 4 slips of paper).

Object of Game:
To reinforce the fruit of the Spirit and affirm family members (or other players) by identifying the characteristics of the fruit of the Spirit that are evident in their lives.

To Play:

1. Place a basket or bowl in front of each player.

2. Pass out slips of paper and pencils. Each player should have one slip of paper for each of the other players. (For instance, if there are five players, each player should have four slips of paper.)

3. Review together the fruit of the Spirit: love, joy, peace, patience, kindness, goodness, faithfulness, gentleness, and self-control.

4. Each player should think of which characteristics of the fruit of the Spirit they see in other players' lives. Each player should silently select one for every other player. Try to use as many of the characteristics as there are players. For example, don't select *love* for all the other players. Select faithfulness for one who is good at keeping promises, kindness for one who does thoughtful deeds for others, joy for one who often has a smile on her face, and patience for one who does not lose his temper easily.

5. Draw a picture of a fruit on each slip of paper. Label the fruit with the characteristic that you have selected for each person.

6. When everyone is finished with their slips of paper, you will take turns filling up each other's fruit baskets. Select the person who will go first (let's say you chose Mom). Mom doesn't say or do anything while her fruit basket is being filled. All the other family members take turns displaying the fruit that they selected to represent Mom. Each person shows his slip of paper and tells why they selected that characteristic for Mom.

7. Go around the circle, doing the same for each family member, until everyone's fruit basket is filled.

It is the duty of all Nations to acknowledge the providence of Almighty God, to obey his will, to be grateful for his benefits, and humbly to implore his protection and favor.

George Washington, 1732-1799

LAND OF LIBERTY
Independence Day

It was not exactly a surprise. The family had received numerous threats from the KGB—not to mention the discrimination they suffered. They were refused jobs and educational opportunities. Finally their worst nightmare came true.

The Ukrainian pastor, his wife, and their fifteen children huddled around a crackling radio, straining to hear the religious broadcast from the free world. The radio pastor spoke words of encouragement as he preached on Revelation 2:10: "Do not be afraid of what you are about to suffer. I tell you, the devil will put some of you in prison to test you, and you will suffer persecution for ten days. Be faithful, even to the point of death, and I will give you the crown of life."

It seemed as if the Lord were speaking directly to Vladimir Khailo and his family. They fell down on their knees in prayer. No sooner had they gotten back up from their time of prayer, than the KGB burst through the door.

Khailo was arrested and subsequently committed to a psychiatric hospital, having been diagnosed as suffering from "religious schizophrenia." In the "hospital," he was used as a guinea pig for various experimental drugs, designed to force him to recant his faith. Over and over he was threatened that, unless he turned away from Christ, his sons also would be imprisoned as they came of age.

For nearly seven years, Khailo did not see his children. When his wife was allowed to visit him, they were kept at opposite sides of the room with a KGB agent between them. Three of his sons were in fact arrested. One was sentenced to a psychiatric hospital, and two were sentenced to prison terms of ten and fourteen years.

Thanks to the prayers and letters of thousands of American Christians, Pastor Khailo was released by the Soviet government and allowed to emigrate with his wife. They live in the United States now and have a deep appreciation for the freedom that they now enjoy. For nine members of the Khailo family, however, the nightmare is not over. Four of the sons and their families remain in the Soviet Union, two of them in prison.

This true story is not an isolated incident. Christians around the world suffer persecution and death for the sake of Christ. Few governments anywhere in the world allow the religious liberty that we possess.

INTRODUCTION

Background

It was religious persecution that drove the first settlers to the shores of this new land. The Pilgrims sought exile on the forlorn New England coast because they desperately desired religious freedom.

Many of our founding fathers were devout Christians. They prized religious liberty as perhaps our most fundamental freedom.

George Washington, the father of our country, was a committed Christian. He began each day on his knees. His writings are replete with references to the "Almighty God" and the "Ruler of the nations."

One of the foremost framers of our Constitution, James Madison, was also a devoted Christian and student of the Bible. The books of Moses, the Pentateuch, provided some of the groundwork for the principles of government on which our country was founded.

These facts are all but ignored in contemporary American life. Many public schools do not even allow God's name to be mentioned for fear of lawsuits. Never mind that He had something to do with the founding of our country!

The burden of education is upon Christian parents, then. We must instill in our children an awareness of what Christians in other lands suffer at the hands of godless governments. We must teach them to cherish our freedom to worship and obey God. Unless it is carefully guarded, that freedom may one day no longer be ours.

Overview

The nation of Israel enjoyed freedom to worship God for many years under the reigns of Saul, David, Solomon, and their successors. But God's people began to compromise their convictions. Their morals went downhill. Finally God's judgment fell, swift and sure. Nebuchadnezzar's armies ransacked Jerusalem and carried off many of the inhabitants to Babylon.

Among the captives were four godly young men, Daniel, Shadrach, Meshach, and Abednego. They were subjected to standard brainwashing techniques (Daniel 1) to inculcate them to the ways of the Babylonians. Daniel's wise handling of this situation provides the basis for the first of three family times, slated for July 1-3.

God blessed their faithfulness and placed them in positions of great influence in the Babylonian, and later Medo-Persian, empires. Nonetheless, they often found their faith at odds with the law of the land. Two such incidents are discussed in the remaining two family times.

This glimpse at the life of Daniel should inspire our faith and foster our appreciation of our own religious liberty. We may also look to Daniel's example when we find our faith targeted by our enemies.

Specific Instructions

The family project for this unit is a Land of Liberty Mural. The only preparation necessary is obtaining butcher paper or a large piece of posterboard for the mural, as well as construction paper. Other materials should be on hand.

A second project idea is to begin praying for Christians undergoing persecution in other countries. You can receive specific information and prayer requests upon writing the address given.

The activity for Independence Day is a surprise picnic, followed by fireworks, building on the traditional July Fourth celebration.

FAMILY PROJECT

Land of Liberty Mural

Materials

- Roll of butcher paper or large piece of posterboard
- Pushpins or masking tape (for hanging mural)

One or more of the following:

- Crayons
- Colored markers
- Paints (Tempera or poster paints)
- White and colored construction paper, glue, and scissors

Instructions

1. Unroll butcher paper or place posterboard on a good writing surface, such as a large table or smooth floor.

2. Have the family draw a landscape depicting our country. Let the children come up with the ideas. (It may include mountains, hills, fields, lakes, rivers, ocean, forests, etc.) Sketch this with pencil, giving everyone an opportunity to contribute.

3. Add buildings and scenes that represent the various freedoms we enjoy. (For example, a school building represents the freedom of education—everyone in our country has an opportunity to get an education.) Sketch these in pencil as well.

4. Leave room for three additional scenes, which your family will add as a part of the three family times of this season.

5. Use crayon, markers, and/or paints to color the mural.

6. Hang the mural on a wall at a level at which everyone in the family can see it.

Using the Land of Liberty Mural

During the family times of this season, we will continue to consider the freedoms that our country affords us. At the conclusion of each family time, we will add another scene to the Land of Liberty mural.

These additional scenes may be drawn and colored directly onto the mural itself. It may be more convenient, however, to make these scenes out of construction paper. The scene can then be glued onto the mural in a vacant spot.

You may draw the additional scenes on white paper, then color or paint them and cut them out. Or you may use variously colored pieces of construction paper to create your scenes.

The final product will be a colorful mural displaying many aspects of our country and our government for which we can be thankful. Independence Day is then a celebration of the freedoms that God has graciously allowed us in this land of liberty.

Other Ideas

As an on-going family project, begin to pray for persecuted Christians in other countries. For names and information on these families, write to Christian Response International, Box 24042, Washington, D.C. 20024. This excellent organization was instrumental in securing the release of the Khailo family. CRI publishes a monthly newsletter with news about Christians facing oppression around the world.

Besides gaining a better appreciation for our own liberty, your children will be encouraged in their faith as they see God answer their specific prayers. And they will begin to understand the worldwide nature of the body of Christ.

FAMILY TIMES AROUND GOD'S WORD

July 1— Captured!

Explain:

After the days of King David and his son, King Solomon, God's people started to disobey God. The Jewish people began to worship false gods and idols and do all sorts of wrong things. God sent prophets to tell the people that if they were sorry and came back to Him, He would forgive them. But the people ignored the prophets. Finally God had to punish His people. He knew that that was the only way they would listen to Him and start to worship and obey Him again.

God allowed the armies of another country, Babylon, to fight against Israel and win. The Babylonians captured many of the Jews and brought them to Babylon.

One of the Jews who was captured and brought to Babylon was a young man named Daniel. He and his three friends, Shadrach, Meshach, and Abednego, were different than many of the other Jews. They loved and obeyed God. But they suddenly found themselves in a country where they were not free to worship and serve the Lord as they had been able to in Israel.

Read:
Daniel 1

Discuss:

1. Daniel and his friends were no longer free to do what they wanted to do. What did King Nebuchadnezzar make them do?

2. It may seem strange that Daniel didn't want to eat the food from the king's table. This was because the food had first been an offering to idols, the false gods of Babylon. Daniel and his friends didn't want to eat something that had been a part of idol worship. What does this tell you about Daniel and his friends?

3. How did Daniel get out of eating the king's food?

4. There may come a time in your life when you will be told to do something that you know is wrong. Your teacher may ask you to read something that teaches things that are against the Bible. Your boss may ask you to lie about something. How can you follow Daniel's example in these situations?

Memorize:
1 Peter 2:17

"Show proper respect to everyone: Love the brotherhood of believers, fear God, honor the king."

Pray:

Heavenly Father, thank You for the country that we live in, where we are free to worship and obey You. Help us to respect and obey our leaders. If we are ever asked to do something wrong, give us the courage and wisdom to know what to do, as Daniel did. In Jesus' name. Amen.

Sing:

"My Country, 'Tis of Thee" (*HWC* 571)

> Our fathers' God, to Thee,
> Author of liberty,
> To Thee we sing:
> Long may our land be bright
> With freedom's holy light;
> Protect us by Thy might,
> Great God, our King. Amen.

Do:

What was one of the freedoms that Daniel and his friends no longer had when they were taken to Babylon? Do we have this freedom in our country? Draw a picture about this on construction paper. Color and cut it out. Glue it onto your Land of Liberty Mural.

July 2 — A Dangerous Choice

Explain:

Because Daniel was so wise, King Nebuchadnezzar made him the ruler over part of his kingdom, including the city of Babylon. Daniel lived in the king's palace and helped the king make many decisions. Daniel made his friends leaders in the Babylonian countryside.

While Daniel was busy doing his job at the palace, King Nebuchadnezzar built something in the countryside which caused big problems for Shadrach, Meshach, and Abednego.

Read:

Daniel 3

Discuss:

1. What was the law that Nebuchadnezzar made about the statue?

2. Why didn't Shadrach, Meshach, and Abednego obey the law?

3. What did they say to the king? How did the king react?

4. What happened to Daniel's three friends after they were thrown into the furnace? Who was the fourth person in the furnace and why was He there?

5. What do you like about Shadrach, Meshach, and Abednego? How can you be like them?

Memorize:

Acts 5:29

"Peter and the other apostles replied: 'We must obey God rather than men!'"

Pray:

Dear Lord, thank You for the courage of Shadrach, Meshach, and Abednego. They obeyed You even though it meant being thrown in the fiery furnace. Help me, Lord, to obey You and stand up for You when I am with people who don't know You. In Jesus' name. Amen.

Sing:

"God of Our Fathers" (*HWC* 573)

> Thy love divine hath led us in the past,
> In this free land by Thee our lot is cast;
> Be Thou our ruler, Guardian, Guide, and Stay;
> Thy Word our law, Thy paths our chosen way.

Do:

As Christians, we base our lives and our beliefs on God's Word, the Bible. Our government is based on something written, too — the Constitution of the United States. This was written in the early days of our country. It sets up how our government should work. One of the most important parts of the Constitution is the First Amendment, which protects our freedom to worship God.

The kingdom of Babylon did not have a Constitution or a First Amendment. Shadrach, Meshach, and Abednego were told to worship a statue instead of the true God.

In many countries around the world today, people are not free to worship God as we are. They must keep their Bibles hidden, and they have to meet secretly for their church services. Aren't you thankful that we are free to worship and obey God in our country? We must remember to pray for our Christian brothers and sisters in other countries whose lives are in danger because they love God.

Draw a picture to represent our freedom of religion. (It may be a Bible, someone praying, a church building, etc.) Color and cut it out. Glue it to your Land of Liberty Mural.

July 3 — A Nasty Trick

Explain:

Daniel continued to love and obey God for many years. Several kings came and went, yet Daniel seemed to stay close to the throne. By the time this story takes place, Daniel is an old man. Darius the Mede is king in Babylon, and Daniel is one of his trusted friends and helpers. Darius decides to make Daniel the ruler over all the other leaders. The other leaders don't like this one bit.

Read:

Daniel 6

Discuss:

1. The other leaders watched Daniel very carefully. They tried to catch Daniel doing something wrong, but they couldn't. What does this say about Daniel? What kind of a person was he?

2. What did Daniel do every day? Do you think that had anything to do with what kind of a person he was?

3. What did Daniel do when he heard about the new law? Why do you think he didn't close his windows?

4. Sometimes people won't like us because we do what is right. We may even be punished for doing what God wants us to do. What should we do if this happens?

Memorize:
1 Samuel 12:24

"But be sure to fear the Lord and serve him faithfully with all your heart; consider what great things he has done for you."

Pray:
Lord God, You do such great and wonderful things. We praise You for being such a mighty God. Help us always to obey You, no matter what people may say or do against us. In Jesus' name we pray. Amen.

Sing:
"What a Friend We Have in Jesus" (*HWC* 435)

What a Friend we have in Jesus,
All our sins and griefs to bear!
What a privilege to carry
Everything to God in prayer!
O what peace we often forfeit,
O what needless pain we bear,
All because we do not carry
Everything to God in prayer!
Have we trials and temptations?
Is there trouble anywhere?
We should never be discouraged;
Take it to the Lord in prayer.
Can we find a friend so faithful,
Who will all our sorrows share?
Jesus knows our every weakness;
Take it to the Lord in prayer.

Do:
Daniel was a man of prayer. Because he spent time thanking God and asking God for help, he was given wisdom to know what to do in difficult situations. We need to become people of prayer, too. Prayer is also important to keeping our nation great and free.

Draw a picture of someone praying (or simply praying hands). Color and cut it out. Glue it onto your Land of Liberty Mural.

FAMILY CELEBRATION

The traditional activity for Independence Day is to have a family picnic, then go watch fireworks. This is a tradition worth perpetuating. But here are some ideas to enhance your family's outing.

Family Picnic

Preparation

The preparation is more than half the fun, in the case of this family picnic. Assign each member of the family one dish to prepare for the picnic. (Little ones will need help, of course, but should know that this is their own project.)

Several days before Independence Day, everyone should decide what he or she will make. Keep these things a secret, so that it will be a surprise at the picnic. Kids love surprises! Then take a trip to the grocery store. Each person should shop for the ingredients for his or her dish.

Then each family member must prepare his or her dish so that it is ready on the Fourth. Give each member of the family as much free rein in the kitchen as is safe and possible (this will take great discipline on the part of "helping" Mom!).

Here are several Independence Day recipe ideas:

Red, White, and Blueberry Gelatin

Ingredients

- 1 package strawberry-flavored gelatin
- 1 container non-dairy whipped topping
- fresh or frozen (thawed) blueberries, washed and well-drained

Directions

Prepare gelatin according to the directions given on the box. Make sure that you prepare it in plenty of time to become very firm. (It is best to make it the day before you serve it.) Thaw the non-dairy whipped topping according to the directions on the container. Just before serving the gelatin, spread the whipped topping on top of the gelatin. Put the blueberries on top of the gelatin. Serve and enjoy!

American Flag Sheet Cake

Directions

Prepare the cake mix of your choice in a jelly roll pan or 9-inch × 13-inch cakepan. Bake according to box directions, and let cool.

Prepare your favorite white or butter frosting. Divide into thirds — place three portions in separate bowls. To the first bowl of frosting, add red food color and stir, adding additional food color one drop at a time, until you achieve red colored frosting. To the second bowl, add blue food color. Do *not* add food color to the third bowl of frosting.

When the cake is cool to the touch, frost the cake with the red, white, and blue frosting in the design of the American flag.*

The Picnic

If you haven't already, find an out-of-the-way spot that can be your special family picnic spot. This place will hold many special memories for your children in the years to come.

Enjoy your surprise picnic together. Be sure to praise the efforts of each child as he unveils his creation.

Play some fun family games like tag, hide-and-seek, or Red Rover. Baseball and Frisbee are good picnic sports if the ages and abilities of your children allow.

Fireworks

Did you know where the American tradition of fireworks on the Fourth came from? In England, fireworks were entertainment enjoyed only by the nobility. In America, fireworks were

---

*For more recipes for kids, try these cookbooks: *New Junior Cookbook*, Better Homes and Gardens, 1979, ed. Gerald Knox, Des Moines, p. 10. *The Little House Cookbook*, by Barbara M. Walker (Harper & Row: New York, NY, 1979).

displayed for all to see on the anniversary of our country's independence. This was a way of celebrating the importance of every individual person in our country. Ours was to be the land of opportunity, for everyone, no matter what his rank or birth. (Of course, all laws regulating fireworks should be respected and safety precautions should be carefully observed.)

Other Alternatives

1. Have a parade. Let each person dress up as one of the founding fathers (or mothers, such as Betsy Ross or Dolly Madison). Make your own drum corps with pots and pans. Carry flags and parade around your neighborhood.

2. For school-aged children, have each person find out about one of our founding fathers. Each person can share what he or she discovered at the family picnic.

The world is so full of a number of things,
I'm sure we should all be as happy as kings.

Robert Louis Stevenson, 1850-1894
"Happy Thought"

SIX

A LONG, LONG JOURNEY

Family Vacation

Evening settled sleepily over the Judean countryside. The flickering light of campfires punctuated the gathering darkness.

What a fun, busy day it had been, reflected David as he watched the fires dance on the dark hillside. The now peaceful setting had been alive with activity as families had been preparing for the Feast of the Tabernacles. Children had laughed and played as they helped gather sticks and boughs. Even baby Hannah had toddled back and forth clutching sticks in her two chubby fists. David had helped his father bind the branches together. Finally, after many dismal failures (which prompted shouts of laughter from the rest of the family), their lean-to was finished. It was just a small shelter, sleeping room only, but it would serve its purpose.

David joined his family around the campfire. Mama cradled a sleeping Hannah in her lap, and Judith was badgering Papa with questions.

"But why are we doing this, Papa? What does it mean?" she asked insistently.

Papa smiled. "That is a good question, little one. Perhaps your big brother can answer."

"When God gave Moses the Law, He instructed him to celebrate three feasts a year: the Feast of Unleavened Bread, the Feast of Harvest, and the Feast of Ingathering. This is the third feast, the Feast of Ingathering, which we celebrate when we gather in the crops from the orchards and vineyards," David explained proudly. Having just turned twelve, he was now considered a man. He would be accompanying his father the next morning to the temple in Jerusalem for the sacred assembly. All the men of Israel would appear before the Lord and the priest would make the offering to God. This would mark the beginning of the seven-day festival.

"But why do we build these huts?" Judith persisted.

"We build these booths, or tabernacles, to remember how our forefathers lived in the desert for eighty years," David continued.

Papa gathered Judith in his arms.

"You see, my little lamb, we live in a wonderful land, a land that the Lord promised to our father Abraham many, many years ago. And here we are, enjoying the figs and the grapes, and all that this land gives us," Papa said. "But this land did not always belong to us. The Lord brought our people out of slavery in Egypt into the desert. There our fathers lived in tents and crude huts like this for eighty years. The Lord wants us to remember this so that we realize something very important: it is the Lord who gave us this good land. It is He who gives us the fruit that we are now gathering in."

"I think I understand now, Papa," Judith replied with a yawn.

David's thoughts turned to the next day's trek to Jerusalem. How exciting that would be! And spending the next seven nights in their little shelter—what fun! As David gazed up at the stars sprinkled across the velvety sky, he felt glad that he was one of God's chosen people.

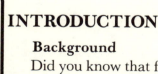

INTRODUCTION

Background

Did you know that family camping is Biblical? God gave the Jewish nation instructions for this annual family camping week known as the Feast of the Tabernacles. This seven-day camping experience had several purposes, one of which was to commemorate the wilderness wanderings of the Israelites.

If your family vacation involves camping, you too have a perfect opportunity to identify with the Israelites and their time in the wilderness. Perhaps your family vacation will not be quite so rugged! Nonetheless, that family time away from home, traveling (with all the unique problems that accompany family trips), presents many parallels to the trek of the Israelites.

Basic to the Feast of the Tabernacles is the principle that family fun and adventure go hand in hand with spirituality. The fun and frolic of building stick shelters was as much a part of the celebration as was the sacred assembly in the temple. When the Lord is truly worshiped, fun becomes holy and holiness is fun. There is no distinction.

Overview

This chapter takes your family on the journey through the desert, from the Israelites' departure from Egypt to the edge of the promised land. It includes ten family times and one time of family worship (for a Sunday morning during vacation), as well as several games and projects appropriate for family vacations.

We can surely identify with Moses and the children of Israel. Together they dealt with the issues of complaining, forgetting, respect, anger, forgiveness. These are not Old Testament problems. We all experience these each day. And the problems are sometimes intensified on a family vacation. As we turn to God's Word for guidance in handling these situations, we find that our family vacation is more spiritual—and much more fun!

Specific Instructions

Several of the projects involve some pre-vacation preparation, such as buying a scrapbook or going to the library. The preparation is minimal, however, and well worthwhile.

Two games are included that can be played in the car on a long (or short) trip. The first is "Where Am I?" a guessing game for the end of the trip, incorporated in Day Ten's activity. The second is an alphabetical memory game, called "I'm Traveling to the Promised Land." This is appropriate at any time during the trip. You can find this game in the Family Celebration section of this chapter.

Musical tapes can provide diversion during tedious travel hours. Christian bookstores offer many children's tape series with fun characters and up-beat praise songs. I would like to recommend one series in particular: "God's Word for Today's Kids," a musical Scripture memory series featuring G. T. and the Halo Express. The characters are delightful, and the songs are Scripture verses (*NIV*) put to music. Many of the Scripture memory verses from this book are put to music in these tapes.

FAMILY PROJECT

Vacations can have their trying moments. Boredom is the frequent complaint of tired children, whether on a long car trip or at a cottage on a rainy day. To help alleviate this problem, three projects are offered here.

The first of these projects ties in with the family times—a vacation scrapbook. Some of the family times involve making things to add to the scrapbook. The second project builds on the theme of Moses and the Israelites in the wilderness. The third project involves developing a theme for your family vacation.

Vacation Scrapbook

Materials

- Scrapbook
- Paper
- Crayons or markers
- Tape
- Scissors
- Camera and film
- Pencils
- Maps

Instructions

This project is an on-going project, done bit-by-bit throughout the vacation. Before the vacation, you will need to purchase the scrapbook (or make one out of construction paper and brads) and assemble all the other materials. Pack all the project materials in one backpack, bag, or small box, and put it in a place that will be accessible during the trip.

Some of the family times will include an activity (e.g., drawing a picture, making a map, etc.) that can be put in the vacation scrapbook.

Fill the rest of the pages with mementos of your vacation. Photographs, travel brochures, objects of nature, all have a place in your vacation scrapbook.

Be sure to write down any funny incidents and include these accounts in your scrapbook. This is a good activity for school-age children as they ride in the car. Have them write down events and incidents from the trip. Encourage them to use their senses — what did they smell, hear, feel, taste, see?

You may want to keep a log of the activities of each day of your trip. This can provide the structure for the scrapbook. Day One would have the log of activities, as well as any photos or other mementos from that day's events.

Family vacations create memories for a lifetime — for you and your children. A vacation scrapbook can preserve these memories for years to come.

The Feast of the Tabernacles

Model Encampment

In the fall of every year, the Israelites remembered the years they wandered in the desert by celebrating the Feast of the Tabernacles, or the Feast of Booths. Families went out and made shelters out of branches and tree boughs. They lived in these "booths" for seven days, while they gathered in the fruit harvest. They did this so that they could understand what it was like for their forefathers to live in temporary shelters for eighty years in the desert.

Can you imagine what it was like — all those Jewish families, with tiny children and old grandparents, together gathering sticks and boughs? They must have had lots of fun making their shelters.

You can try the same thing. But instead of making a full-sized shelter, make a model.

Materials
- Twigs and small sticks
- Glue

- Straw or dried grass
- Paper

Instructions

Decide where you will construct your model encampment. If you build it outdoors you will need a sheet of plastic to protect it from rain and stones to anchor down the plastic. If you build it indoors (a good rainy day activity, if you have a good spot to work), you will need a piece of cardboard, a box, or a sheet of posterboard for a base for your encampment.

Break the twigs and sticks into appropriate lengths and construct little huts. You may want to make the walls individually, by gluing a row of sticks as they lie flat on the table. After the walls dry, they may be assembled (like a prefabricated house!). Make roofs out of sticks or straw glued on paper. Make your encampment as elaborate or as simple as you like.

Vacation Theme

Decide on something you would like to learn about as a family on this vacation. Your theme will be determined to a certain extent by where you are going and what you are doing. When you have selected your theme, go to the public library and check out a few books that can serve as references or learning aids as you explore your theme. Here are a few examples:

1. Your family will be camping in the Smoky Mountains. You decide that you want to learn about the trees in that part of the country. You go to the library and check out a guidebook on trees of the Appalachian region or the Southeastern United States. When your family goes hiking, you bring along the guidebook and try to figure out what all the different trees are by examining their leaves, bark, and the like. Keep a notebook of all the different trees you encounter.

2. Your family is visiting Boston, Massachusetts. Find a book or two on the American Revolution (check with the children's librarian for books appropriate to the age of your children). As you travel, read aloud any interesting, pertinent information about Boston and the events that happened there during that

historic period. As you visit historic locations, recall what happened there. Write down any impressions or new insights.

3. Your family will be spending a week at the Pacific Ocean. You decide to learn about the tides. Find a book that explains tide action in simple terms. Then learn by actual experience. Mark the high tide. When the tide is low, measure the distance between high and low tide.

4. Birdwatchers have a built-in theme wherever they go! All you need is a field guide and a pair of binoculars. Keep a record of all the birds you spot.

FAMILY TIMES
AROUND GOD'S WORD

Day One — God Leads
His People

Explain:

Why is your family taking a vacation? There are probably several reasons. One reason is to take a break from work and the regular routine, to have some relaxing family time. We are going to be looking at a very long trip that God's people, the Israelites, took. They desperately needed a break — a big one!

The Israelites were slaves in Egypt. That means that they had to work hard for little or no money, and they were not free to quit or move away. Their masters were cruel to them and beat them. God heard their cries and their prayers and answered them. He chose Moses to lead them out of Egypt to a wonderful land — Canaan — the land that He had promised Abraham many years before.

But the king of Egypt, Pharaoh, didn't want to let the Israelites go. God sent many bad things to Pharaoh so that he would change his mind. Only when God's angel killed Pharaoh's oldest son did he let the Israelites go. God told Moses to have the people ready so that they could leave quickly, before Pharaoh changed his mind again.

There were about two million Israelites that started out on that long trip in the middle of the night. Can you imagine what it was like, all those people getting ready to leave? The worst of it was, they didn't even know where they were going or how to get there! They just knew that God told them to leave.

Read:
Exodus 13:17-18, 20-22

Discuss:
1. When you left on your trip, how did you figure out where you were going? The Israelites didn't have maps or travel agents. How did they know where to go?
2. Why didn't God lead them the short way?
3. God wants to lead us just as He led the Israelites. To follow God means to do what He wants us to do in the choices we make each day. How can we know what God wants us to do?
4. If the Israelites had been planning the trip, they would have taken the short road. It was really only a short way to Canaan. Instead, God led them the long way around — it took them forty years to get to Canaan, when it could have only taken several years. God led them this way because He had many things to teach them in the wilderness. Also, He didn't want them to have to fight the people who lived in the land of the short road.

God knows what is best for us. He can see things that we can't see when we are making decisions. That is why it makes sense for us to trust and follow Him and read and seek to understand His Word. What can you do to help yourself remember to follow Jesus?

Memorize:
Proverbs 3:5-6

> "Trust in the Lord with all your heart
> and lean not on your own understanding;
> in all your ways acknowledge him,
> and he will make your paths straight."

Pray:
Heavenly Father, You are such a great God! You know everything. And You care about me and want to lead me on the

right road every day. Help me to follow You by obeying Your
Word. In Jesus' name. Amen.

Sing:

"Guide Me, O Thou Great Jehovah" (*HWC* 51)

> Guide me, O Thou great Jehovah,
> Pilgrim through this barren land;
> I am weak, but Thou art mighty,
> Hold me with Thy pow'rful hand;
> Bread of heaven, Bread of heaven,
> Feed me till I want no more,
> Feed me till I want no more.

Do:

Draw a map of the route that you are taking on your trip.
Write at the top of the page, "I am following Jesus." Mount this
on the first page of your family vacation scrapbook.

Day Two — Problems, Problems!

Explain:

The Israelites had hardly gotten started when they ran into
big problems. Has your family run into problems yet? It will
probably happen, sooner or later. No matter how bad our problems seem, they can't begin to compare with the problems that
the Israelites faced.

Read:
Exodus 14:1-31

Discuss:

1. What problem did the Israelites face at the very beginning of their trip? What did they say to Moses?

2. How did Moses answer them?

3. What did God tell them to do?

4. How did God save the Israelites?

5. When the Israelites saw God's great power, what did they
do (v. 31)?

6. You will probably run into problems on your family vacation. When you do, what should you try to remember?

Memorize:
Psalm 46:1

> "God is our refuge and our strength,
> an ever-present help in trouble."

Pray:
Heavenly Father, Your power is so great! You saved the Israelites in such a mighty way. We know that You can work out our problems in a mighty way, as well. Help us to remember to trust You instead of becoming worried and upset. In Jesus' name. Amen.

Sing:
"God of Our Fathers" (*HWC* 573)

> God of our fathers, whose almighty hand
> Leads forth in beauty all the starry band
> Of shining worlds in splendor thru the skies,
> Our grateful songs before Thy throne arise.

Do:
Write on a slip of paper what you want to remember when a problem comes up. Mount this in your vacation scrapbook, leaving room for a photo. When a problem comes, a flat tire, a spilled Coke, a motel with no vacancies, or other unforeseen mishaps, take a picture that you can mount under your reminder. This way, you can look at problems as opportunities to trust the Lord.

Day Three — Bitter to Sweet

Explain:
Do you ever get thirsty when you are driving in the car on a long trip? How about on a long hike? How would you feel if you couldn't have anything to drink for three whole days?

Read:
Exodus 15:22-27

Discuss:

1. What did the Israelites do when they couldn't find any good water to drink? Was that good or bad? What should they have done?

2. What did Moses do? What did God do?

3. What is "grumbling"? Do you ever grumble? Does it make your parents happy when you grumble? What do you think God thinks of grumbling?

4. Think of that bitter water as a problem in your life. When we pray, often God doesn't take our problem away, but He turns it into something that can be used for good. Just like He made the bitter water sweet. Can you think of a problem that God has turned into something good?

Memorize:

Psalm 34:10

> "The lions may grow weak and hungry,
> but those who seek the Lord lack no good thing."

Pray:

Father, thank You that You are good, and all good gifts come from You. Help me to pray instead of grumbling. In Jesus' name. Amen.

Sing:

"God of Our Fathers" (*HWC* 573)

> Refresh Thy people on their toilsome way
> Lead us from night to never-ending day;
> Fill all our lives with love and grace divine,
> And glory, laud, and praise be ever Thine.

Do:

Buy a box of soda crackers and eat as many as you can. Don't drink anything. Wait for half an hour before you have anything to drink. As you wait, talk about what it was like for the Israelites in the hot desert without anything to drink for three days.

Day Four—I'm Starving!

Explain:

Do you ever ask your parents, "When is it going to be lunchtime?" Do you ever complain that you are starving or beg for a snack at a gas station? When you're traveling, it seems that all you can think about is food! The Israelites felt the same way, only worse. There wasn't any fast food in the desert—only sand, sand, and more sand!

Read:
Exodus 16:1-18

Discuss:

1. What were the Israelites grumbling about?
2. Who did Moses say they were really complaining against? Why did he say that?
3. What did the Lord do?
4. When we complain to our parents, who are we really complaining against? Should our parents be as gracious as God was to the children of Israel? Is it always wrong to complain? Why?
5. Just as God gave the Israelites what they needed, not more, not less, He has promised us that He will provide for us. How can this help us not to complain?

Memorize:
Philippians 4:19

"And my God will meet all your needs according to his glorious riches in Christ Jesus."

Pray:

Dear Lord, we have so many good things that come from Your hand—our family, health, safety, home, and food. Help us to remember that You always take care of us. In Jesus' name. Amen.

Sing:

"All People That On Earth Do Dwell" (Old Hundredth) (*HWC* 20)

Know that the Lord is God indeed;
Without our aid He did us make;
We are His folk, He doth us feed,
And for His sheep He doth us take.

Do:

Write a list of all the good things that God has given you. You may limit it to blessings you have received while on vacation, or you may make it more general. Think of a title for your list and mount this in your scrapbook.

Day Five—Please Give Me a Hand

Explain:

As if traveling through the desert weren't bad enough, now the Israelites found themselves being attacked by a group of people called the Amalekites. Moses chose a young man named Joshua to lead the Israelite men in battle. He knew that his place was not on the battlefield. Moses had a more important job to do.

Read:
Exodus 17:8-15

Discuss:

1. Where did Moses go during the fighting? Why?

2. Why do you think God made the Israelites win when Moses' hands were up and lose when he dropped his hands?

3. What happened when Moses' hands or arms got tired?

4. How can we be like Moses when we have problems and struggles? What does God want us to do?

5. Sometimes we get tired or sick or discouraged. At times like that, it is hard to pray. What should we do when we are having a hard time praying or obeying?

Memorize:
Psalm 46:1

"God is our refuge and our strength,
an ever-present help in trouble."

Pray:

Father, You are so great that there is no problem too difficult for You. Help me to remember to come to You with my problems and seek the counsel of reliable friends, and to keep praying, even though it takes a long time to see Your answer. Thank You for giving us Christian friends who can pray for us and talk with us and encourage us when we are tired and discouraged. In Jesus' name. Amen.

Sing:

"What a Friend We Have In Jesus" (*HWC* 435)

> Have we trials and temptations?
> Is there trouble anywhere?
> We should never be discouraged:
> Take it to the Lord in prayer.
> Can we find a friend so faithful,
> Who will all our sorrows share?
> Jesus knows our every weakness;
> Take it to the Lord in prayer.

Do:

Have each person think of one special friend with whom they can share their problems, who can pray for them. Write down the name and/or draw a picture of this special Christian friend.

Day Six — Thunder Mountain

Explain:

Have you ever been in a very frightening thunderstorm? What frightened you the most? Today we will read about a very special thunderstorm.

Read:

Exodus 19:3-9, 16-19

Discuss:

1. How did God come to Moses? Why (v. 9)?
2. Close your eyes and try to imagine what it was like when God came in the thunderstorm on the mountain (vv. 16-19).

Describe what you see. How would you feel if you were one of the Israelites?

3. God called Moses up on the mountain to give him the Law. He was going to tell Moses all the things that the Israelites should and shouldn't do. One of the reasons God came in such a loud, powerful thunderstorm was to show the people that He was there, and He was telling Moses what to write down. Moses wasn't just making it up himself. What did God tell Moses that He would do if the people obeyed Him (vv. 5, 6)?

4. Do you think that it is important for us to obey God? Why?

Memorize:

Isaiah 41:10

"So do not fear, for I am with you; do not be dismayed, for I am your God. I will strengthen you and help you; I will uphold you with my righteous right hand."

Pray:

Holy Father, You are a mighty God. Even the loudest, most frightening thunderstorm is nothing compared to Your great power. Yet You love us and have made us Your own — Your treasured possession. Thank You for Your love. Help us to honor and obey Your Word. In Jesus' name. Amen.

Sing:

"O Worship the King" (*HWC* 10)

O worship the King, all glorious above,
O gratefully sing His power and His love;
Our shield and defender, the Ancient of Days,
Pavilioned in splendor, and girded with praise.

O tell of His might, O sing of His grace,
Whose robe is the light, whose canopy space;
His chariots of wrath the deep thunderclouds form,
And dark is His path on the wings of the storm.

Do:

Draw a picture of the thunderstorm on the mountain.

Day Seven — God Gives the Law

Explain:

Does your family have rules? What are some of them? When Moses went up on the mountain, God gave him some rules for the Israelites, God's family. The most important of these rules are called the Ten Commandments.

Read:

Exodus 20:1-21

Discuss:

1. Discuss what each of the Ten Commandments means.

2. The first four Commandments have to do with respecting God. The last six have to do with respecting other people. What does it mean to respect someone? Why is this so important?

3. Do you always show respect for the other members of your family? What sorts of things do you do that are disrespectful? What can you do differently?

4. What can you do to give God the respect that He deserves?

Memorize:

John 14:21a

"Whoever has my commands and obeys them, he is the one who loves me."

Pray:

Heavenly Father, You deserve our respect, our worship, everything we have. Help us to honor You in everything we do and say. Help us to show respect for others, especially those in our own family. In Jesus' name. Amen.

Sing:

"O Word of God Incarnate" (*HWC* 269)

O Word of God incarnate,
O Wisdom from on high,
O Truth unchanged, unchanging,
O Light of our dark sky,

We praise Thee for the radiance
That from the hallowed page,
A lantern to our footsteps,
Shines on from age to age.

Do:

If you were going to find ten rules for your family to live by, what would they be? Write down your family's own "Ten Commandments" and mount this in your scrapbook.

Day Eight — A Terrible Sin

Explain:

Have you ever heard the expression, "When the cat's away, the mice will play"? When Moses came down from the mountain, he found that the Israelites, like naughty children, had gotten into no end of trouble.

Read:
Exodus 32

Discuss:

1. What did the Israelites do when Moses took too long in coming down from the mountain? What did God want to do to the Israelites?

2. How did Moses feel when he saw the calf and the dancing? What did he do?

3. Even though Moses was terribly angry with the people, he prayed for them, asking God not to destroy them. Read his prayer in verses 31 and 32. What did he offer to do?

4. Moses could not die for the Israelites' sin, because he, like the Israelites, was sinful. Only the death of God's perfect Son, Jesus Christ, could remove sin. God answered Moses' prayer and didn't destroy the Israelites, but He did punish them. What were their punishments?

5. When Moses saw the people running wild, what did he call out in verse 26? Have you ever done something so bad that you thought that God could not forgive you? We all feel like that sometimes. When we do, we need to remember that: (1) Jesus

died in our place—our sin is taken away. When we ask for forgiveness, our sin is taken and buried at the bottom of the deepest sea, no matter how bad it was; and (2) God is always calling us to come back to his side, just as Moses called.

Review:
Proverbs 3:5-6

Pray:
Dear Lord, please forgive me for the times that I have forgotten about You or done wrong things. Thank You that because of Jesus' death on the Cross, You forgive me and take away my sin. Next time I am in the middle of sinning, help me to stop sinning and to obey you. In Jesus' name. Amen.

Sing:
"Who Is On the Lord's Side?" (*HWC* 484)

> Who is on the Lord's side?
> Who will serve the King?
> Who will be His helpers
> Other lives to bring?
> Who will leave the world's side?
> Who will face the foe?
> Who is on the Lord's side?
> Who for Him will go?
> By Thy call of mercy,
> By Thy grace divine,
> We are on the Lord's side,
> Savior, we are Thine.

Do:
Write down on a slip of paper a sin that you have done. Don't show anyone, but pray silently, asking God to forgive you for that particular sin. Then thank God for forgiving you, as He has promised. Then take the slip of paper and rip it into tiny pieces. Burn it in your campfire or throw it in the wastepaper basket. This reminds you that God has forgiven that sin and forgotten it.

Day Nine — A Fatal Flare-up

Explain:

Do your parents ever lose their temper? Every parent does — even Moses, who was like a parent to the children of Israel. Even so, it is still wrong. Today we read about a time when Moses' temper tantrum had terrible consequences.

Read:

Numbers 20:1-13

Discuss:

1. What was the problem in verses 2-5? What were the people doing again?

2. Moses started out doing the right thing. He went to God and prayed about the problem. What did God tell him to do? Did Moses obey Him? What did Moses do?

3. What was Moses' punishment for disobeying God? It happened just as God said it would. He let Moses look at the land of Canaan, but He did not let Moses go into the land.

4. Do you think that this was a hard punishment for Moses? God said that He was punishing Moses because Moses "did not trust in Me enough to honor Me as holy in the sight of the Israelites (v. 12)." When Moses hit the rock, he did not show respect for God. He acted as if he didn't believe that God could bring water out of the rock in the way that He said He would. Also, the people probably thought that it was Moses who brought water out of the rock. Moses said, "Must we bring water out of this rock (v. 10)?"

5. Sometimes when God wants us to do something, we "sort of" obey Him. We do something like what He wants us to, but we do it in our own way. Do you think there is such a thing as "sort of" obeying? Why does this make God unhappy?

Review:

Proverbs 3:5-6

Pray:

Heavenly Father, we are sorry for losing our tempers and for doing things our own way, instead of obeying You. Forgive us, and help us to remember to honor You. In Jesus' name. Amen.

Sing:

"All People That on Earth Do Dwell" (*HWC* 20)

> O enter then His gates with praise;
> Approach with joy His courts unto;
> Praise, laud, and bless His Name always,
> For it is seemly so to do.
> For why? the Lord our God is good:
> His mercy is for ever sure;
> His truth at all times firmly stood,
> And shall from age to age endure.

Do:

Find a rock and a stick. Place these out somewhere as a reminder to obey God and not to lose your temper.

Day Ten—The Final Farewell

Explain:

Moses was not the only one who was punished by not being allowed to enter Canaan. When the Israelites finally got to the promised land, and they saw the strong people that lived there, they became worried and frightened. They were afraid that they would all be killed. Only two people besides Moses, Joshua and Caleb, trusted in God and believed that God would help them to win.

God was very disappointed that after all the great things He had done for the Israelites, they still didn't trust Him. So He said that they would not be allowed to go in. They would have to spend another forty years wandering in the desert. Can you imagine? Only their children, and Joshua and Caleb, would be allowed to go into the new land.

It was at the end of this second forty years, when Israel was about to enter the promised land, that God told Moses that it was time for him to die. Before Moses climbed Mt. Nebo, where he was to die, he gave one last message to the Israelites. He recited a song about God's greatness, and His love and faithfulness. Then he told them to be sure to obey God.

Read:
Deuteronomy 32:44-47, 34:1-12

Discuss:

1. What did Moses say about obeying God? How important was it for the Israelites to obey God?

2. Moses said of God's commands, "They are your life (v. 47)." Is God's Word that important to you? What can you do to make it more important in your life?

3. God kept His promise not to let Moses enter the new land because Moses disobeyed Him. But God did answer Moses' prayer and let him see the new land. How do you think Moses felt when he looked out and saw the land that he had been trying to get to for eighty years?

4. How did Moses die? Who buried him?

5. What do the last three verses say about Moses? Would you like to be like Moses? In what way?

Memorize:
Deuteronomy 31:6(b)

> "The Lord your God goes with you;
> he will never leave you nor forsake you."

Pray:
Father, You are gracious and good. Thank You for caring for us, just as You cared for Moses and the Israelites. We sin and complain and lose our tempers just as they did, yet You forgive our sin. Because of Jesus, we can one day enter heaven. We thank and praise You, Lord, in Jesus' name. Amen.

Sing:
"Guide Me, O Thou Great Jehovah" (*HWC* 51)

> When I tread the verge of Jordan,
> Bid my anxious fears subside;
> Death of death and hell's destruction,
> Land me safe on Canaan's side;
> Songs of praises, Songs of praises,
> I will ever give to Thee,
> I will ever give to Thee.

Do:

Remember together all the good things that the Lord has done for you on your vacation. As a fun way of recapping the events of your trip (and to find out what was memorable to your children), play the following game:

Game: "Where Am I?"

This game is a variation on "Twenty Questions." The object of the game is to guess the place selected by the person who is "it."

Each person takes a turn being "it." This person thinks of a particular place from the experiences of the family during the vacation. The rest of the family tries to guess the place by asking the person questions which can be answered by yes or no.

For example, Tommy, who is "it," remembers the ice cream parlor in Bar Harbor, where he got a double scoop of Rocky Road, and Suzy dropped her ice cream cone on the floor. The family asks yes-no questions until they discover what Tommy is thinking.

FAMILY CELEBRATION

Vacations often present the opportunity for family worship. Worship is a celebration of who God is and what He has done. The following family celebration includes a format for family worship, focusing on Moses' face-to-face encounters with God. The goal of this time is to draw the family into a face-to-face encounter with the glory of God.

This family celebration also includes a game that reinforces what the family is learning about the experiences of Moses and the Israelites in the wilderness.

Family Worship

Call to Worship:

Leader 1:

I will proclaim the name of the Lord.

Oh, praise the greatness of our God!

He is the Rock, his works are perfect,
    And all his ways are just.
A faithful God who does no wrong,
    upright and just is he (Deuteronomy 32:3, 4).

Sing:

"Praise, My Soul, the King of Heaven" (*HWC* 3)

Praise, my soul, the King of heaven;
To his feet thy tribute bring;
Ransomed, healed, restored, forgiven,
Who like me His praise should sing?
Alleluia! Alleluia!
Praise the everlasting King.
Praise Him for His grace and favor
To our fathers in distress;
Praise Him, still the same forever,
Slow to chide, and swift to bless:
Alleluia! Alleluia!
Glorious in His faithfulness.

Read:

Psalm 136 (responsively)

Leader 1:
Give thanks to the Lord, for he is good.

All:
His love endures forever.

Leader 2:
Give thanks to the God of gods.

All:
His love endures forever.

Leader 1:
Give thanks to the Lord of lords:

All:
His love endures forever.

Leader 2:
To him who alone does great wonders,

All:
His love endures forever.

Leader 1:
Who by his understanding made the heavens,

All:
His love endures forever.

Leader 2:
Who spread out the earth upon the waters,

All:
His love endures forever.

Leader 1:
Who made the great lights,

All:
His love endures forever.

Leader 2:
The sun to govern the day,

All:
His love endures forever.

Leader 1:
The moon and stars to govern the night;

All:
His love endures forever.

Leader 2:
To him who struck down the firstborn of Egypt

All:
His love endures forever.

Leader 1:
And brought Israel out from among them

All:
His love endures forever.

Leader 2:
With a mighty hand and outstretched arm;

All:
His love endures forever.

Leader 1:
To him who divided the Red Sea asunder

All:
His love endures forever.

Leader 2:
And brought Israel through the midst of it,

All:
His love endures forever.

Leader 1:
But swept Pharaoh and his army into the Red Sea;

All:
His love endures forever.

Leader 2:
To him who led his people through the desert,

All:
His love endures forever.

Leader 1:
Who struck down great kings,

All:
His love endures forever.

Leader 2:
And killed mighty kings,

All:
His love endures forever.

Leader 1:
Sihon king of the Amorites,

All:
His love endures forever.

Leader 2:
And Og king of Bashan,

All:
His love endures forever.

Leader 1:
And gave their land as an inheritance,

All:
His love endures forever.

Leader 2:
An inheritance to his servant Israel;

All:
His love endures forever.

Leader 1:
To the One who remembered us in our low estate

All:
His love endures forever.

Leader 2:
And freed us from our enemies,

All:
His love endures forever.

Leader 1:
And who gives food to every creature.

All:
His love endures forever.

Leader 2:
Give thanks to the God of heaven.

All:
His love endures forever.

Read:
Exodus 33:12-23

Read:
Mark 9:2-8

Discuss:
1. What did Moses pray for? Why?
2. What was God's answer?
3. Why wasn't Moses allowed to see God's face?
4. Did Moses ever see God's face? When?
5. The Bible tells us that God has shown Himself to us in Jesus (Colossians 1:15-20). Jesus shows us exactly what God is like. Do you want to see God face-to-face, as Moses did? How can we do that?

Pray:
Holy Father, we praise You for Your glory. Thank You for showing Yourself to us in Jesus. Because of His death on the Cross, we can know You and speak to You face-to-face, as Moses did. In Jesus' name we pray. Amen.

Sing:
"Immortal, Invisible" (*HWC* 25)

> Immortal, invisible, God only wise,
> In light inaccessible hid from our eyes,
> Most blessed, most glorious, the Ancient of Days,
> Almighty, victorious, Thy great Name we praise.

Great Father of glory, pure Father of light,
Thine angels adore thee, all veiling their sight;
All praise we would render: O help us to see
'Tis only the splendor of light hideth Thee. Amen.

Family Fun

"I'm Traveling to the Promised Land"
Number of Players:
3-30

Length of Time:
15-30 minutes

Object of the Game:
To remember all the items named.

To Play:
Players take turns saying "I'm traveling to the promised land, and on the way, I'll need _____." The first person fills in the blank with an item beginning with the letter A.

The next player repeats exactly what the first said, but adds an item beginning with the letter B. Each subsequent player goes through the entire list, adding an item beginning with the next letter in the alphabet.

If someone forgets an item, the penalty is that he must spend one more year wandering in the wilderness. The winner is the player with the least number of years of wilderness wandering by the end of the alphabet.

People were bringing little children to Jesus to have him touch them, but the disciples rebuked them. When Jesus saw this, he was indignant. He said to them, "Let the little children come to me, and do not hinder them, for the kingdom of God belongs to such as these. I tell you the truth, anyone who will not receive the kingdom of God like a little child will never enter it." And he took the children in his arms, put his hands on them and blessed them.

Mark 10:13-16

SEVEN

FEARFULLY AND WONDERFULLY MADE

Birthdays

My almost-six-year-old stood at my right elbow, watching eagerly, as I guided the fabric through the sewing machine.

"When is my flag going to be finished, Mom?" she asked for the hundredth time.

"Pretty soon," came the reply. "I'm on the last letter now."

"Can I help?" she asked.

"Let's see, you can help me iron the applique on," I said as I pulled the fabric out and snipped the threads.

Together we set up the iron, and together we counted to ten as we heated the nylon fabric to receive the applique. We switched off the iron, turned over the flag, and voila! Laura's birthday flag was complete.

"Shall we give it a test fly?" I suggested.

Laura's eyes sparkled as we raced downstairs. She slipped the flag onto the flagpole, and we marched outside. The wind caught the brilliant purple standard and hurled it straight out so that the white letters danced all in a row—L-A-U-R-A.

Laura looked up at me with excitement and affection.

"I'm so glad I have a birthday flag, Mom," she said. "That makes me feel special! Can we fly it all month?"

INTRODUCTION

Background

Something has happened to birthdays. What used to be an occasion for an intimate family celebration has become big business. Children's parties get bigger and more extravagant every year, with dozens of children, expensive outings, clowns, and bulging goodie bags.

These parties are exciting and sensational, no doubt, but do they really make the birthday child feel important? Many a guilty parent has his conscience assuaged by these expenditures. Yet it is like acquiring material wealth—no matter how much you get, it's not enough. Next year's party has to be bigger, better, more exciting. But are the child's deepest needs satisfied?

Every child has a need to feel loved and valued. Birthdays are an especially important time to meet this need. A birthday is a holiday in which one person is celebrated. That person is honored and shares the day with no one else (except in the case of twins or triplets). Even grown-ups feel the need to be honored, especially on their birthdays. How much more keenly do children feel it!

How does one go about honoring someone? Throwing a lot of money in his direction lends a temporary thrill, but does not give that person an abiding sense of worth. The things that we do and say are far more important in instilling in that person the sense that we respect and honor him.

Children's parties can contribute to making a child's birthday a wonderful memory and a time when they feel honored. They are no substitute, however, for a family celebration in which the family honors the birthday child. The child's peers come to a party interested primarily in themselves and the fun that they will have. Only the child's family loves that child enough to put his interests first. Parents especially can honor the child in a way that no one else can.

The purpose of this chapter is to give parents a format for honoring their child on his or her birthday. Birthdays are perhaps the most important days of the year to children. The memories, good or bad, last a lifetime. Christian parents want to make memories of fun, loving family times, grounded in God's Word. This chapter will enable you to celebrate your child's birthday in a way that will make him feel special and loved, by his family, and more important, by God.

Overview

Four family times are included in this chapter, one per birthday. The family time around God's Word can take place at breakfast on the child's birthday or after the birthday dinner.

The focus of this time is our value to God. Each family time looks at one aspect of our relationship to God. The underlying principle is that our lives have value because of God and what He has done on our behalf.

The four actions that God has taken that make up the four family times are: (1) God chose us, (2) God created us, (3) God redeemed us, and (4) God called us. Each of the Scripture passages demonstrates that God values us and has a plan and purpose for our lives.

These principles are crucial ones to instill in our children. We want their sense of worth to come from who they are in God's sight, not from who they are in the distorted perspective of society. No one can measure up to the world's standard of beauty, brains, and bucks. Such values leave everyone feeling inadequate. We want our children to stand firm and confident in the assurance of God's unconditional love.

Specific Instructions

Directions are given for making a birthday flag or banner. This is a visible, tangible way to honor your child and to announce to the world that this is his special day. Let your child choose the colors of the flag or banner.

Several suggestions are offered for making the birthday a day-long family celebration. These include "King or Queen for a Day," a family birthday outing, and a family birthday celebration.

This does not preclude having a children's party in addition to the family celebration. The children's party should be on a different day, however. Perhaps you will decide to give a children's party every other year, instead of every year. Let wisdom rather than peer pressure be your guide.

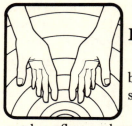

FAMILY PROJECT

What better way to honor a child on his birthday than to fly a special flag or hang a special banner that represents who he is?

Instructions are given for two options: an outdoor flag and an indoor banner. Those who sew will want to choose the outdoor flag, which involves machine stitching. Others may opt for the indoor banner, which requires a minimal amount of sewing.

If your home is not equipped with an outdoor flagpole, don't be dismayed. The materials list includes an inexpensive flagpole stand that is easily mounted on the outside of your house. You need not buy a flagpole; you can simply buy a dowel as specified in the materials list.

If you do have a legitimate flagpole in your yard, you will skip buying the flagpole stand and dowel. Instead, you will buy grommets to apply to your flag, so that you can hook it onto your flagpole.

The indoor banner is similar in concept to the outdoor flag, but it is made of materials that are not weatherproof. The component parts are glued, for the most part, rather than sewn.

Birthday Flag

Materials

- Two brown paper grocery bags
- Background fabric: 3 feet × 5 feet brightly colored nylon or cotton (child's favorite color)
- Contrasting fabric: 1 yard (for letters of child's name)

    or

- 1 yard of heavy-weight iron-on interfacing (non-woven, preferable). See Step #7 in Instructions for Making Flag.
- Thread to match background fabric
- Trim: 5⅜ yards contrasting trim (optional)
- Flagpole: 1 rod, ¾-inch diameter, 6 feet long
- Flagpole holder for ¾-inch flagpole

Instructions

1. If you bought cotton fabric, preshrink the fabric by machine washing in hot water. Tumble dry and iron. Nylon need not be preshrunk.

2. Finish the edges of the background fabric. Fold raw edges in ¼ inch. Fold again and machine stitch.

3. Make casing for flagpole. Fold one of the 3 foot sides in 1½ inches. Machine stitch ¼ inch from inside edge. Stitch the top of the casing closed, as shown in Figure 7A.

   OR

   If you already have a flagpole that uses hooks and grommets, install grommets in the corners of one of the 3 foot sides of the flag. (Follow the directions on the package for installing the grommets.)

4. If desired, sew contrasting trim to the "right" side of the flag around its perimeter and along the casing seam, as shown in Figure 7B.

5. Make patterns for the letters of the child's name out of the grocery bags. (For a five-letter name, the letters would be about 16 inches high by 10 inches wide. Size will vary with the length of the child's name.)

6. Pin patterns to the contrasting fabric (or iron-on interfacing) and cut out letters.

7. Applique the letters to the right side of the flag. (If your sewing machine does not do applique stitches, then finish the raw edges of the letters and simply sew around the perimeter of the letters to attach them to the flag.)

   OR

   If you are using iron-on interfacing instead of fabric, simply follow the directions that come with the interfacing for applying the interfacing to the flag background. The letters will be permanently affixed to the background without having to sew them on.

8. Applique on the flag any other figures or symbols representing your child and his or her interests or achievements.

9. Slide flagpole into casing. The top end of the casing, which is sewn closed, will hold the flag on the end of the flagpole.

10. Attach flagpole holder to outside of house. Insert flagpole in flagpole holder.

Using the Birthday Flag

Every year, applique one or more figures to the flag that represent interests, achievements, or special events from the previous year.

Fly the flag all day on the child's birthday. Also, fly the flag on other days that are special for your child. For instance, if your son wins the spelling bee at school, put his flag out to honor him.

Birthday Banner

Materials

- Felt sheets, 8-½ inches × 11 inches, one for each letter in the child's name, in a color that will contrast with the background color.

- Felt background, ½ yard wide, length determined by number of letters in child's name. (For a five-letter name, 55 inches would be taken up by letters. A 60-inch length would be the minimum.)

- Appliques or felt scraps to make figures to glue onto banner.

- Tacky glue (glue for fabrics)

- Thread to match background

- Decorative trim for banner (optional)

- 1 dowel, ⅝-inch diameter, 20 inches long

- 1 length of cord, ⅛-inch diameter, 36 inches long

Instructions

1. Fold top edge of banner over to the back side 1½ inches (see Figure 7C).

2. Sew overlap one inch from fold and ½ inch from edge, as shown in Figure 7D. This forms the casing for the dowel.

3. Make patterns for the letters of your child's name on sheets of 8½ inch × 11 inch paper (one letter per sheet of paper, so that the letters are about 8½ inch × 11 inch in size).

4. Cut out patterns and pin them to felt sheets. Cut out felt letters.

5. Glue felt letters to banner as shown in Figure 7E.

6. Using felt scraps or other fabrics or materials, make figures representing interests or achievements of the child. Glue these to the banner.

7. Decorate the banner, if desired, with decorative trim. (For instance, glue or sew gold braid around perimeter of banner.)

8. Drill a hole in the dowel ¾ inch from each end (see Figure 7F). If a drill is not available, use Option 2 in Step 10.

9. Insert dowel into casing.

10. *Option 1*
    Stiffen ends of cord by wrapping with tape. Draw ends of cord through holes at ends of dowel and knot or tie cord (see Figure 7G).

    Option 2
    Tie cord around ends of dowel. Glue cord to dowel so that cord will not slide toward the center when hung (see Figure 7H).

Using the Birthday Banner

Every year, glue one or more figures to the banner that represent interests, achievements, or special events from the previous year.

Hang the banner in a prominent place on the morning of the child's birthday. You may also want to hang the banner on other days that are special for your child.

Figure 7A

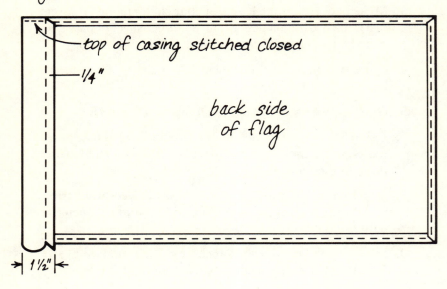

top of casing stitched closed

—1/4"

back side
of flag

|← 1½" →|

Figure 7B

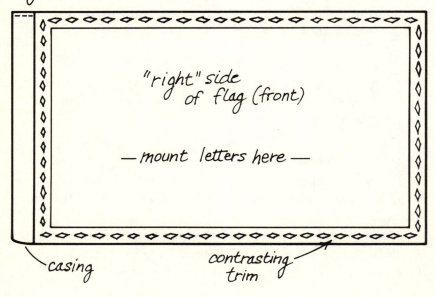

"right" side
of flag (front)

— mount letters here —

casing

contrasting
trim

Figure 7C

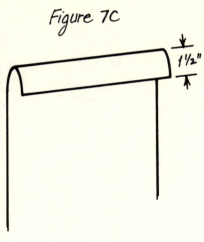

1½"

Figure 7D

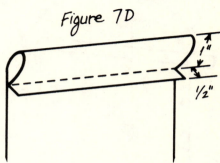

1"

½"

Figure 7E

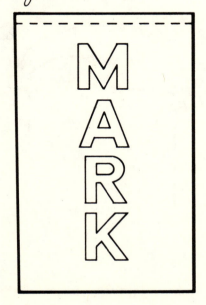

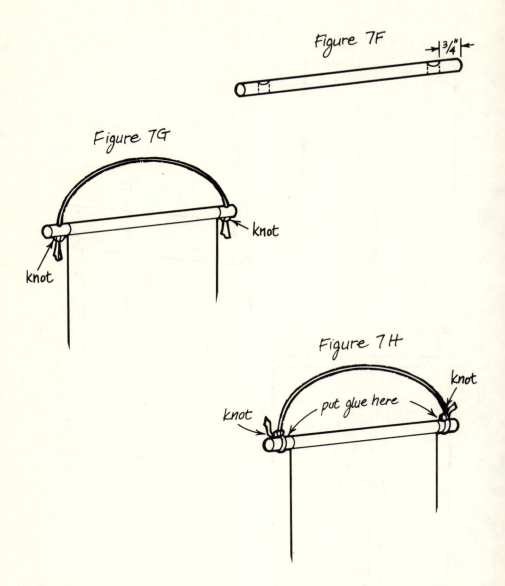

Figure 7F

3/4"

Figure 7G

knot

knot

Figure 7H

knot

put glue here

knot

FAMILY TIMES AROUND GOD'S WORD

Birthday #1 — God Chose You

Explain:

Do you know someone who is adopted? Perhaps you are adopted. If so, that is especially wonderful because of what it shows us about God's love. The Bible tells us that all those who are His are His by adoption.

Read:

Ephesians 1:4-6

Discuss:

1. When did God choose us? Predestined means "decided ahead of time." What did God decide ahead of time for us? Why?

2. What did God have in mind for us? (Read v. 4 again.)

3. When you think about God choosing you before He even created the world, how does that make you feel?

4. We should want to praise God for His goodness (see v. 6). It is because of Jesus' death on the Cross that we receive all these good things from God and are adopted as His children. Can you think of a time when it would be especially important for you to remember that you are chosen by God and His special child?

Memorize:

1 John 3:1(a)

"How great is the love the Father has lavished on us, that we should be called the children of God! And that is what we are!"

Pray:

Heavenly Father, we praise You for choosing us and adopting us as Your own children. We know that it is not because of our goodness, but it is because of Your goodness and grace.

Help us to always remember who we are and that we belong to You. In Jesus' name. Amen.

Sing:

"Children of the Heavenly Father" (*HWC* 44)

> Children of the heavenly Father
> Safely in His bosom gather;
> Nestling bird nor star in heaven
> Such a refuge e'er was given.
> God His own doth tend and nourish,
> In His holy courts they flourish.
> From all evil things He spares them,
> In His mighty arms He bears them.

Do:

Tell what being God's child means to you (have everyone share).

Birthday #2 — God Created You

Explain:

Are there some things about you that you would change if you could? Perhaps it is your nose, or your ears, your hair, or your knobby knees. Clothing designers are the people who create the fashions we wear. The greater the designer, the more expensive his clothes are. Did you know that you were fashioned by the greatest Designer in the universe?

Read:

Psalm 139:13-16

Discuss:

1. What do these verses tell us about how we were made?

2. When you value something, that means that it is important to you. From these verses, do you get the idea that God values us? Why?

3. Verse 16 says that all our days are written in God's book. That means that our whole life is important to God, and every single day counts to Him. How does it make you feel when you think about this?

Memorize:
Psalm 139:14

"I praise you because I am fearfully and wonderfully made; your works are wonderful. I know that full well."

Pray:
Dear Lord, thank You that You care so much about each one of us. Thank You that You made each of us different, and You love each of us so very much. When other people hurt us, or don't care, help us to remember how important we are to You. In Jesus' name. Amen.

Sing:
"The King of Love My Shepherd Is" (*HWC* 468)

> The King of love my shepherd is,
> Whose goodness faileth never;
> I nothing lack if I am His,
> And He is mine forever.
>
> And so through all the length of days
> Thy goodness faileth never;
> Good Shepherd, may I sing Thy praise
> Within Thy house forever.

Do:
Write out verse 14 and tape it to your mirror.

Birthday #3 — God Redeemed You

Explain:
Long ago, many poor people were not free. They were sold to rich people. They couldn't go where they wanted to go or do what they wanted to do. They were slaves and had to do exactly what their master said.

Imagine what it would be like to be born to a slave family. As a young boy or girl, your master might sell you to someone else. You would be separated from your parents and could never be with them again. And what if your new master were cruel? What if he beat you? This happened to many slave children.

The Bible tells us that actually everyone born into this world is born into a kind of slavery — and the master is sin. That means that we don't do what is right and don't think to love and know God. We do what our master, sin, tells us to do.

But God doesn't want us to be slaves. He wants us to be free. But in order for us to be set free, we needed to be bought from our master, sin. Someone needed to pay the price for us. These verses tell us who paid for us, so we could be set free, and what had to be paid.

Read:
1 Peter 1:18-19

Discuss:

1. To redeem someone means to free them from something bad by paying a price. Who paid for us to be set free?

2. What did He pay?

3. Which is more precious to God: gold and silver, or His Son?

4. If God paid such a high price for you, what does that tell you about how important you are to Him?

5. What do you think is the most valuable thing in the world? The world's largest diamond, perhaps? Yet there is nothing about a diamond that makes it more valuable than an ordinary rock. What makes it valuable is the amount of money that people are willing to spend on it. In the same way, what makes us valuable is the price that God was willing to pay for us.

Memorize:
Romans 5:8

"But God demonstrates his own love for us in this: While we were still sinners, Christ died for us."

Pray:
Dear Lord, thank You for paying the highest price ever — Your own life and blood — to buy us away from sin. Thank You that we are valuable to You. Thank You that we are free to love and obey You, instead of having to mind the cruel master, sin.

Help us to live our lives like free people, not like slaves to sin. In Jesus' name. Amen.

Sing:

"Savior, Like a Shepherd Lead Us" (*HWC* 462)

> Savior, like a shepherd lead us,
> Much we need Thy tender care;
> In thy pleasant pastures feed us,
> For our use Thy folds prepare:
> Blessed Jesus, Blessed Jesus,
> Thou hast bought us: Thine we are.
>
> Thou hast promised to receive us,
> Poor and sinful though we be;
> Thou hast mercy to relieve us,
> Grace to cleanse, and power to free:
> Blessed Jesus, blessed Jesus,
> Early let us turn to Thee.

Do:

Act out the redemption of a slave and talk about how that relates to Jesus redeeming us.

Birthday #4 — God Called You

Explain:

Do you sometimes wish that you were someone else? Or do you sometimes feel that you just aren't "good enough"? Everyone feels that way sometimes.

God doesn't want us to feel stuck in that pattern, though. In His Word, He tells us that each of us is special to Him. He has a plan for each of us if we are willing to obey Him.

One day, God spoke to a man named Jeremiah. God wanted Jeremiah to be His prophet, to give His message to the people of Israel. Read God's words to Jeremiah and see if they offer you any insight into God's plan for you.

Read:

Jeremiah 1:4-10

Discuss:

1. When did God first know Jeremiah? When did He decide that Jeremiah would be His prophet?

2. What did Jeremiah say? How was he feeling?

3. What did God say and do to give Jeremiah the confidence that he needed?

4. When did God first know you? Do you think that He made you with a specific purpose in mind?

5. How can you know what God wants you to do and be? What should you remember if you are afraid?

Memorize:

Jeremiah 29:11

" 'For I know the plans I have for you,' declares the Lord, 'plans to prosper you and not to harm you, plans to give you hope and a future.' "

Pray:

Thank You so much, Father, for knowing us before we were even formed. Thank You for making each of us with something special in mind. Today we thank You especially for _____ and the special person that You have created him (her) to be. You have a plan for his (her) life, Lord, and a reason for everything about him (her). Help him (her) to remember this, and to remember that You will always be with him (her). In Jesus' precious name. Amen.

Sing:

"Take My Life and Let It Be" (*HWC* 379)

Take my life, and let it be
Consecrated, Lord, to Thee;
Take my moments and my days,
Let them flow in ceaseless praise.

Take my love; my Lord, I pour
At thy feet its treasure-store;
Take myself, and I will be
Ever, only, all for Thee.

Do:

Have each member of the family name one thing about the birthday child that is special or that they especially appreciate.

FAMILY CELEBRATION

Children don't need to be told that their birthday is a special day. They know it! Perhaps the parents' greatest challenge is creating a birthday celebration that meets the child's lofty expectations.

Here are some suggestions for making the family birthday celebration festive and memorable. For the sake of simplicity, let us call the birthday child Sara.

King or Queen for a Day

From the moment Sara wakes up on her birthday, she is given special honor in the family. She is "Queen for a Day." She is given a construction paper crown to wear and is given the seat of prominence at the breakfast table.

The meals that day consist of her favorite foods. Either she has been allowed to select the menus for the meals, or Mom has made what she knows to be Sara's favorite foods. Sara is looking forward to enjoying her very favorite dinner for her family party that evening.

One of the best things about Sara's birthday is how Mom and Dad make a big deal of her. Usually they are careful to treat all the children with equal attention, but today is different. Today Sara is the most important member of the family, and she loves it!

The phone starts to ring early in the morning with birthday wishes from friends and relatives. Neighborhood friends stop by with homemade cards for Sara. (Sara doesn't know it, but Mom has made a point of telling all her friends that today is her birthday.)

Sara's birthday flag flaps in a gentle breeze, announcing to all who drive by that today is her day. Her name stands out in bright white letters against the dark pink background. The flag makes Sara feel very special.

Birthday Outing

Soon it is time for the family birthday outing. Each child chooses a special place to go for a family outing on his or her birthday. Sara has chosen a park by a lake with a lovely beach area and a fun playground. Mom packs a picnic lunch, loads the kids in the car (giving Sara the front seat, of course), and off they go. Although the family often goes to this park, today it is special, because Sara chose it.

(Other birthday outing ideas include: museums, nature walks, historic buildings, sports events, boat trips, or activities such as roller skating, bowling, horseback riding, ice skating, and the like.)

Birthday Celebration

Dinner is served in the dining room tonight on the good china. Everyone comes to dinner all dressed up, and Sara is the guest of honor. She is seated at the head of the table. When they ask the Lord's blessing on the meal, Dad prays a prayer of thanksgiving for Sara. He thanks God for creating her the wonderful girl that she is. He gives thanks for the good year that she has had and asks God's blessing on the coming year.

After the main course, Dad leads the family in a birthday family time around God's Word. The focus is on God creating each person a unique individual, with unique gifts, and with a special purpose in life. The family affirms Sara's gifts, the things about her that make her special.

Then comes the birthday cake and the presents. Sara goes to bed utterly exhausted and blissfully happy. As she recalls all the events of her day, it seems a glowing blur. Greater than the thrill of getting presents is the joy of being loved and accepted and honored. It has been the best birthday ever.

"I have served Him eighty-six years," replied Polycarp, "and in no way has He dealt unjustly with me; so how can I blaspheme my King who saved me?"

Polycarp, 69-155
when ordered to renounce Christ or die

EIGHT

HEROES OF THE FAITH

All Saints' Day

The hammer struck the nail with several determined, well-placed blows. With fire in his eyes and his jaw set, the young monk turned from the cathedral door, leaving the parchment treatise to flutter in the chill October air.

A passer-by witnessing this scene would have given it scarcely a second thought. Scholars frequently tacked discourses on the wooden doors of the imposing Castle Church in Wittenburg. Written in Latin, such documents invited other scholars to debate and discussion. Martin Luther's Ninety-Five Theses stated his case against the abuses of the Roman Church with the purpose of initiating change within the hierarchy of the church.

When others secretly translated these articles into German and distributed them among the people, the sound of the hammer on the door of Castle Church echoed across all of Germany. Luther himself could not have dreamed that the blows struck that Eve of All Saints, 1517, would still resound five centuries later.

INTRODUCTION

Background

Halloween, we call it, from All Hallow's Eve or All Saints' Eve. Children love the ritual of dressing in costume and marching from door to door collecting goodies. "Trick or treat!" they cry, their words somewhat muffled by the grotesque masks covering their faces. All year long, they plan what they will dress up as next Halloween.

Some schools spend the better part of October emphasizing Halloween themes—witches, ghosts, jack-o'-lanterns, and black cats are the subjects of stories and crafts. The reason for this seems apparent. Fearful of "civil liberties" lawsuits, public schools avoid "religious" holidays altogether. The absence of Christmas and Easter creates a huge void, which teachers seek to fill with secular holidays and themes. Halloween is perceived as "religiously neutral," and witches and ghosts are seen as imaginary creatures that children enjoy. It is all merely fun—perfectly innocent.

Or is it? On this particular night of the year, vandalism runs rampant. Incidents of razor blades and drugs found in children's treats have become so frequent that many hospitals offer free x-raying of Halloween candy. Few stop to ask the question, "Why do so many horrible things happen on Halloween?"

Perhaps the answer lies in the origin of the holiday. Halloween finds its roots in the pagan cultic rites of the ancient Celtic people. The Vikings were a Celtic people, as were the ancient inhabitants of Ireland, Scotland, Wales, and Germany. Their high priests, called Druids, taught worship of things in creation, earth, sky, fire, trees, animals, and the like. One of their deities was Samhain, the Lord of the Dead, to whom they paid tribute on October 31, the eve of their new year.

The Druids taught that on this night, the souls of the wicked dead inhabited the bodies of living people to be entertained, placated, and thus appeased. These "possessed" people would go out in the countryside to the farm houses and literally play "trick or treat." If the frightened country folk did not provide suitable food, shelter, and entertainment, they would destroy their property and cast evil spells upon their home. In Wales, ghastly faces were carved in gourds, then the gourds were lighted and carried by the "trick or treaters" to aid in spooking the country people.

So, at its foundation, Halloween is a fiendish celebration of death, a tribute to the wicked spirits of the underworld. It was not widely observed in our country until the late 1800s, when a large number of Celtic peoples immigrated from Europe—people who had never relinquished this yearly observance.

But what is All Saints' Day, and why does it coincide with this pagan festival? All Saints' Day, originally celebrated in May,

was a Christian celebration honoring those who had died in Christ.
When the fingers of the Roman Church reached northward to
Germany and Scandinavia, the church moved the All Saints' celebration to November 1 in order to displace the pagan practices.
The northern tribes still had their October 31 celebration of the
dead, but now it was somehow to be "Christianized." Unfortu-
nately the All Saints' celebration did not completely displace Halloween and in fact the two events gradually became intermingled.

All Saints' Day, in and of itself, is a good and worthy celebration if it is observed in a Biblical manner. Based on Hebrews 12:1
and 1 Peter 5:4, the Episcopal Book of Common Prayer states in
its Preface of All Saints' Day:

> For in the multitude of your saints, you have surrounded us
> with a great cloud of witnesses, that we might rejoice in their
> fellowship, and run with endurance the race that is set before
> us; and, together with them, receive the crown of glory that
> never fades away.

We do not pray to the saints but merely take this occasion to
remember them and thank God for the sacrifices they made in
order that we might know Jesus Christ. It can only enrich our
faith to acknowledge Martin Luther, John Calvin, and John
Knox, giants of the Reformation. At great personal cost, the
Wesleys preached throughout England and the colonies the good
news of salvation by faith in Jesus Christ. Modern "saints" such
as Hudson Taylor, Amy Carmichael, and Jim Elliot poured out
their lives for Jesus in remote corners of the world. This is an appropriate occasion to recall those who directly influenced our
lives for Christ—parents, youth leaders, that special Christian
friend. It is a time of thanksgiving to God for those who have
gone before us, for those who have been faithful unto death.

The purpose of this chapter is to suggest to Christian parents
an alternative to Halloween. Instead of celebrating death, let us
celebrate life by remembering heroes of the faith.

Overview

Hebrews 11 forms the basis for the All Saints' family times. It
is a catalog of heroes of the faith—those who believed God's spe-

cific promises to them despite seemingly insurmountable obstacles. From this list, four heroes have been chosen as examples.

The first family time, celebrated the first week in October, focuses on Noah and the exercise of his faith in the building of the ark. Abraham's obedience to God's call is the theme of the second family time. The subject of the third family time is Joshua and his victory over Jericho. The last week in October, the family will look at one who was small in stature but gigantic in faith—David, as he was pitted against Goliath. None of these four men was perfect, but God exercised their faith so that they can stand as role models for us today.

The corresponding project is a hands-on, kids-only craft. Each child makes a Heroes of the Faith Poster, adding scenes to the poster each week as a new hero is examined.

The culminating celebration is an All Saints' party to replace the Halloween activities. Ideas for costumes, food, games, and stories are provided. Game suggestions include Abraham's Walk of Faith, Eye Spy, Heroes of the Faith Charades, and Hero Interviews, all Biblical adaptations of ordinary party games. Let these ideas stimulate your imagination to create the best kids' party ever—better than Halloween by a long shot!

FAMILY PROJECT

The family project for the month of October is a bit different from those of the other seasons. The children play the primary role in constructing this project. Instead of one project for the entire family, there is one per child.

The project is a Heroes of the Faith Poster for each child to hang in his or her room. Every child needs heroes. This project is aimed at encouraging our children to choose heroic men and women from the Bible to emulate rather than war-mongering characters from Saturday morning cartoons.

The basic background of the poster is simple and can be constructed easily at the beginning of the month. Then, after each family time, a scene depicting a Bible hero is created and added to the poster.

The following instructions are addressed to the children. The children can make this project with minimal assistance from parents.

Materials
- One sheet of posterboard for each child
- Letter stencils (purchased at a drug store)
- Colored markers
- Crayons
- String for hanging poster
- Paper punch
- Glue
- Pencils

Instructions

1. Using a pencil and the letter stencils, trace around the inside of the stencils to make these words at the top of your poster:

HEROES OF THE FAITH
Hebrews 11

2. Color in these letters on your poster with brightly colored markers.

3. Punch one hole in each of the two top corners of your poster. Make the holes far enough in so that they don't rip through to the edge of the poster.

4. Cut a piece of string, 30 inches long. Tie the ends of this string in the holes at the corners of your poster (see Figure 8A).

5. Hang the poster on a nail in the wall of your room. You will be adding colorful scenes to this poster throughout the coming month.

Using the Heroes of the Faith Poster

1. At the end of each family time, you will use either crayons and markers on plain white paper or colored construction paper to make a picture of the Bible story that you just discussed in your family time.

Figure 8A

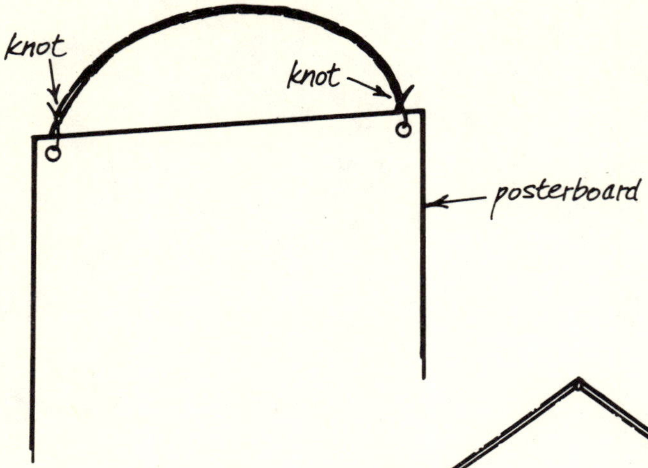

knot

knot

posterboard

Figure 8B

Completed
"Heroes of
    the Faith"
Poster

HEROES OF THE FAITH
Hebrews 11

2. Small children may want to draw and color on white paper, whereas older children may want to cut out figures from construction paper. Or try a combination of the two. Just do whatever you want to create a scene showing the Bible hero in whatever situation he was in from the Bible passage.

3. When you have created your Hero of the Faith scene, glue or tape it to your poster, leaving room for the remaining scenes. There will be four scenes in all (see Figure 8B).

FAMILY TIMES AROUND GOD'S WORD

First Week of October — Noah

Explain:

Have you ever been told to do something that seemed totally ridiculous? Did you do it? That would depend on who told you to do it, wouldn't it? If it were your loving mom or dad, you should do it. If it were the goofy kid down the block, you probably shouldn't.

One day, many years ago, a man named Noah was told to do something that seemed ridiculous. In the part of the world where Noah lived, it hardly ever rains. There were no lakes or oceans anywhere close, perhaps not even a river. What do you suppose Noah thought when he was told to build a huge boat? Now if it had been his neighbor who told him to build it, Noah would probably have laughed. But Noah was given these orders by someone very special.

Read:
Genesis 6:9 - 8:22

Discuss:

1. What did God say to Noah?
2. Did Noah believe God? How do you know?
3. List all the things that Noah did and all the things that God did.

4. How does God "talk" to us today? How can we show that we believe God?

5. Can you think of something else that was made of wood that God used to save people? Even as early as the time of Noah, God was pointing to the day when He would provide a way to save us from our sins. But we have to "go into the ark" by believing what God says about Jesus. We need to receive Jesus as our Savior by believing in what He has done on the Cross.

Memorize:

Proverbs 3:5-6

> "Trust in the Lord with all your heart
>   and lean not on your own understanding;
> In all your ways acknowledge him,
>   and he will make your paths straight."

Pray:

Heavenly Father, thank You that You are a God who saves. Thank You for sending Jesus to die on the Cross for me, so that I could be saved from sin and death. Give me the faith of Noah, to believe You and do exactly what You say to do in Your Word. In Jesus' name. Amen.

Sing:

"A Mighty Fortress Is Our God" (*HWC* 26)

> A mighty fortress is our God,
> A bulwark never failing;
> Our helper He amid the flood
> Of mortal ills prevailing.
> For still our ancient foe
> Doth seek to work us woe —
> His craft and pow'r are great,
> And, armed with cruel hate,
> On earth is not His equal.
>
> Did we in our own strength confide,
> Our striving would be losing,
> Were not the right man on our side,
> The man of God's own choosing.
> Dost ask who that may be?

Christ Jesus, it is he—
Lord Sabaoth His name,
From age to age the same,
And He must win the battle.

And tho' this world with devils filled,
Should threaten to undo us,
We will not fear, for God hath willed
His truth to triumph thru us.
The prince of darkness grim,
We tremble not for him—
His rage we can endure,
For lo, his doom is sure:
One little word shall fell him.

That word above all earthly pow'rs,
No thanks to them, abideth;
The Spirit and the gifts are ours
Thru Him who with us sideth.
Let goods and kindred go,
This mortal life also—
The body they may kill;
God's truth abideth still:
His kingdom is forever.

Do:

Using white paper with crayons or markers, or using construction paper and scissors, create a scene from the story of Noah to put on your Heroes of the Faith Poster. Glue or tape it on your poster when you finish.

Second Week of October—Abraham

Explain:

Has your family ever moved to a new town where you didn't know anyone? What was it like? If you haven't, try to imagine what it would be like.

One day God told Abraham to move. Try to imagine how Abraham felt as you read this story.

Read:
Genesis 12:1-9

Discuss:

1. When God came to Abraham, He said two things. He told him to do something (an instruction) and He told Abraham what He, God, would do (a promise). What was the instruction, and what was the promise?

2. What did Abraham do? Do you think he waited around until he wanted to go, or does it sound like he obeyed right away?

3. When your parents tell you to do something, do they mind if you wait around and do it when you feel like it? When do they want you to obey?

4. Did Abraham know where he was going? How did he know where to go? How do you know what God wants you to do?

5. What did Abraham do when he got to Canaan? He built an altar to worship God and to remember that God had led him to this place.

Memorize:

Hebrews 11:6

"And without faith it is impossible to please God, because anyone who comes to him must believe that he exists and that he rewards those who earnestly seek him."

Pray:

Dear Lord, thank You for giving us the Bible to show us the way that You want us to live. Help us to study it and believe it so that we obey You right away. In Jesus' name. Amen.

Sing:

"The Church's One Foundation" (*HWC* 277)

The Church's one foundation
Is Jesus Christ her Lord;
She is His new creation
By water and the word:
From heaven He came and sought her
To be His holy bride,
With His own Blood He bought her,
And for her life He died.

Elect from every nation,
Yet one o'er all the earth,
Her charter of salvation
One Lord, one faith, one birth;
One holy Name she blesses,
Partakes one holy food,
And to one hope she presses,
With every grace endued.

'Mid toil and tribulation,
And tumult of her war,
She waits the consummation
Of peace for evermore;
Till with the vision glorious
Her longing eyes are blest,
And the great Church victorious
Shall be the Church at rest.

Yet she on earth hath union
With God, the Three in One,
And mystic sweet communion
With those whose rest is won.
O happy ones and holy!
Lord, give us grace that we
Like them, the meek and lowly,
On high may dwell with Thee.

Do:

Using white paper with crayons or markers, or using construction paper and scissors, create a scene from the story of Abraham to put on your Heroes of the Faith Poster. Glue or tape it on your poster when you finish.

Third Week in October — Joshua

Explain:

Do you remember how Moses led the Israelites to the promised land? Moses died before entering the promised land with the Israelites. God chose a new leader for his people. Moses' helper Joshua became the leader of the Israelites.

The promised land was not just open farmland. It had cities and towns with lots of people living in them. The people who lived there were under God's judgment. God told Joshua to go into this land and kill the people. Then the Israelites could live in their cities and towns, harvest their crops, and pick the fruit from their fruit trees. God said this because He wanted to punish the wickedness of the Canaanites and because He had a special plan for His people, the Israelites, to inherit the land of His choosing.

The first city the Israelites came to was Jericho.

Read:
Joshua 6:1-21

Discuss:
1. If you were going to capture a city, how would you do it? What did God tell Joshua to do?
2. What did Joshua think of God's plan? How do you know?
3. How many of God's instructions did Joshua obey? Do you think that it is important to obey all of God's instructions? Why?
4. What happened to the walls of the city? What made the walls collapse? What were some lessons that God was trying to teach the Israelites?

Memorize:
Isaiah 41:10

"So do not fear, for I am with you; do not be dismayed, for I am your God. I will strengthen you and help you; I will uphold you with my righteous right hand."

Pray:
Dear Father, You are so great. There is nothing that is too hard for You. Help me to be like Joshua and believe that You can do anything. Help me to show that I believe You by doing exactly what You say. In Jesus' name. Amen.

Sing:
"How Firm A Foundation" (*HWC* 275)

How firm a foundation, ye saints of the Lord,
Is laid for your faith in His excellent Word!
What more can He say than to you He hath said,
To you who for refuge to Jesus have fled.

"Fear not, I am with thee; O be not dismayed,
For I am thy God, and will still give thee aid;
I'll strengthen thee, help thee, and cause thee to stand,
Upheld by My righteous, omnipotent hand.

"When through fiery trials thy pathway shall lie
My grace, all sufficient, shall be thy supply
The flame shall not hurt thee; I only design
Thy dross to consume and thy gold to refine.

"The soul that on Jesus hath leaned for repose
I will not, I will not desert to its foes;
That soul, though all hell should endeavor to shake,
I'll never, no, never, no, never forsake!"

Do:

Using white paper with crayons or markers, or using construction paper and scissors, create a scene from the story of Joshua to put on your Heroes of the Faith Poster. Glue or tape it on your poster when you finish.

Fourth Week in October — David

Explain:

Many years had passed since the children of Israel entered the promised land. They now had a king, King Saul, and their land was now called Israel. But having their own land, and having their own king, didn't mean that all their problems were over.

The Israelites had terrible neighbors. The Philistines were the people that lived right next to Israel. These people hated Israel and they worshiped false gods. They continually attacked the Israelites to try to get their land.

At that time, a young boy named David worked in the fields as his father's shepherd, and also frequently played the harp for the king. (The king had terrible moods, and listening to David play the harp helped him feel better.) David's older brothers fought in the king's army against the Philistines. Let's see what happened one day to David as he was running an errand for his father.

Read:
1 Samuel 17:1-51

Discuss:

1. What did Goliath shout to the Israelite soldiers? Why did this so upset David?

2. What did David do about it? How did he think that he could beat Goliath?

3. Who else believed that David could beat Goliath? What did other people say to him?

4. What did Goliath say to David? What did David say to Goliath before he loaded up his sling (vv. 45-47)? Even before it happened, David knew that God would give him victory over Goliath. What was the reason that he gave (vv. 46-47)?

5. Although we may never have to fight an angry giant, as David did, we do face problems. Do you sometimes have problems that seem giant-sized? How can David's example help us as we face our problems?

Memorize:

Philippians 4:13

"I can do everything through him who gives me strength."

Pray:

Heavenly Father, You can conquer the biggest problem in our lives. Give us David's faith to trust You and do what is right in spite of the greatest difficulties. In Jesus' name. Amen.

Sing:

"Faith of Our Fathers" (*HWC* 279)

> Faith of our fathers! living still
> In spite of dungeon, fire and sword;
> O how our hearts beat high with joy
> Whene'er we hear that glorious word!
> Faith of our fathers, holy faith!
> We will be true to thee till death!
>
> Our fathers, chained in prisons dark
> Were still in heart and conscience free:
> How sweet would be their children's fate,
> If they like them could die for thee!
> Faith of our fathers, holy faith!
> We will be true to thee till death!

Do:

Using white paper with crayons or markers, or using construction paper and scissors, create a scene from the story of David and Goliath to put on your Heroes of the Faith Poster. Glue or tape it on your poster when you finish.

FAMILY CELEBRATION

All Saints' Party

Children love to dress up in costumes, play games, win prizes, and get lots of goodies. That is why Halloween holds such attraction for them. However, a fun party can incorporate all these elements without the ghosts and witches theme. Any alternative to Halloween needs to be just as much fun—or more so.

Parties are becoming more and more common on Halloween because parents are reluctant to send their children out trick-or-treating in this day of increased violence. Because of this trend, children will not be branded as "weird" for going to an All Saints' party instead of trick-or-treating. If they have more fun and get more goodies than all their friends, they will feel that they got the better end of the stick.

An All Saints' party revolves around Bible heroes, and godly men and women in church history, instead of the evil characters that are generally celebrated on Halloween. Children come to the party dressed up as Bible characters. Animals qualify as Bible characters, from the creation, Noah's ark, and a host of other Bible stories in which animals play a part.

Invite several other Christian families to participate with you in this event. They will be comfortable with the biblical theme and will probably appreciate having an alternative to the usual Halloween activities.

A fun party consists of good friends, good food, and fun activities. This requires some careful planning, but it need not be costly or overly involved. Several suggestions follow that may help you plan your All Saints' party. Perhaps these will spark your imagination to create something that your family will enjoy even more.

1. GOOD FOOD. Spread your table with treats to eat during the party, either throughout the evening (finger foods) or at a specific time (cake and ice cream).

2. GOODIE BAGS. Make sure that each child takes home a goodie bag full of treats so that he doesn't wish that he had been able to go out trick-or-treating. (Most kids evaluate the success of their evening by dumping the contents of their goodie bag on the floor and proceeding to count the various treats.)

3. COSTUMES. Children delight in dressing up. As they make their initial appearances in their costumes, they should each be made to feel that their costume is something special. Avoid contests for best costumes — this leads to disappointment for many.

4. STORY-TELLING. Scour your church or public library for stories of great Christians. Find a story that is the appropriate length and level for the ages of children present, one that will excite and inspire them. Look for such characters as Augustine, Athanasius, Martin Luther, John Calvin, Hudson Taylor, Charles Spurgeon, Lottie Moon, George Mueller, Amy Carmichael, or George Whitefield. *Foxe's Book of Martyrs* is jam-packed with harrowing tales of those who laid down their lives for Jesus Christ. Schedule a "story hour" in the events of the evening and read such accounts dramatically.

5. GAMES. Plan a number of simple, fun party games. These can be ordinary party games, or they can be slightly modified to capitalize on the Bible hero theme. The emphasis here is not on learning (although in some cases learning may result). Rather, the emphasis is on hilarity — just plain fun!

Here are several examples of ordinary party games that have been modified to reflect the theme of Bible characters and events.

Abraham's Walk of Faith
Materials:
    Blindfolds

Location:
Outdoors in yard or indoors, using entire house

Time:
About 10 minutes

Object of the Game:
To learn to trust another person by following his voice without being able to see.

To Play:
Divide the group into pairs. In each pair, one will be the follower and the other will be the leader. The follower puts on a blindfold so that he cannot see anything. First, have the leader spin the follower around so that the follower is disoriented. Then, the leader must lead the follower around the yard or house using only verbal directions. The older the players, the more complex and circuitous route they should take. When the leader has returned to the starting point with the follower, the follower should take off his blindfold. Have the follower guess where he has been. Then switch places, the leader becoming the follower and vice versa.

Note:
Emphasize that it is extremely important for the leader to be trustworthy. All players must be willing and able to lead their partners so that the followers do not hurt themselves. If some of the children are unable to handle this responsibility, use a different game.

Eye Spy

Explain:
There are spies in the Bible! The most famous spy was Joshua, who, with Caleb and ten other spies, scouted out Canaan before the Israelites entered.

Number of Players:
5-25

Time:
15-60 minutes

Materials:
One candle, a dark room, a slip of paper for each player

Object of the Game:
To guess which player is the spy before you are winked at by the spy.

To Play:
On one of the slips of paper, draw an eye. On the other slips of paper, either draw an *X* or leave them blank. Fold up the slips of paper and put them in a bowl or basket.

Have all the players sit in one circle around a lighted candle. Turn out all the other lights. Pass the bowl around and have each player select a slip of paper. The one who selects the slip with the eye on it is the spy.

Once everyone has looked at his slip and folded it back up, playing commences. All players must maintain eye contact with other players at all times during this game. The spy tries to get as many players out as he can before someone guesses that he is the spy. He gets players out by winking at them. Conversely, the players try to guess who is the spy before the spy catches their eye, winks at them, and they are out.

If a player sees another player wink and suspects him of being the spy, he says "Eye Spy!" and indicates who the spy is. The accused spy must show his slip of paper to prove his guilt or innocence. If the guess is wrong, that player is out. If he is right, he wins the game and a second round may begin.

Heroes of the Faith Charades

Number of Players:
Any number

Time:
15-60 minutes

Materials:
A Bible

Object of the Game:
To guess which Bible character is being portrayed by the actor.

To Play:
Each player is given a turn to be the actor. The actor selects a "hero of the faith" either from the Bible or from church history. He has three minutes to convey without words the identity of this character. He can do this by pantomiming scenes from this character's life, or he can use charades techniques to communicate the character's name. (Holding up two fingers means the name has two syllables; cupping the ear means "sounds like . . .", etc.) Other players, of course, must try to guess the character. The person with the right answer takes the next turn unless he has already had a turn. If so, he may give the turn to a person who has not yet been the actor.

Hero Interviews
Number of Players:
Any number

Length of Time:
10-20 minutes

Materials:
A tape recorder and a blank tape

Object of the Game:
To identify with Bible characters and make them come alive by using a "man-on-the-street" interview routine.

To Play:
Each player selects a Bible character to represent. One of the older children is the "roving reporter." (Several may take turns at being the reporter.) Each Bible character is interviewed by the

reporter, who is taping the interview. (It helps if the reporter is a bit of a ham!)

Here is a sample interview:

Reporter:
I have with me today David of Bethlehem, who has just killed Goliath and won a major victory for Israel. Tell me, David, how did you, a shepherd boy, end up fighting against the giant Philistine?

David:
Well, I was bringing some cheese to my brothers, who are in the army. When I got to the battlefield, I couldn't believe my ears. This big bully was calling the Israelites names and making fun of the One True God. I was pretty upset. I told King Saul that I would fight against Goliath and show the Philistines whose God is the real one.

R:
Were you nervous?

D:
Not really. You see, as a shepherd, I've come up against some pretty scary things — lions and bears after my sheep. God has given me the power to fight these beasts with my bare hands and tear them limb from limb. I knew that He would deliver Goliath into my hands.

R:
How did you know that?

D:
I just knew that God wouldn't stand for His name being dragged in the mud by those wicked, filthy Philistines.

R:
I heard that King Saul offered you the use of his armor.

D:

Yeah, that was pretty funny. I put on his armor and it was so heavy, I couldn't move. I would have been a sitting duck in that.

R:

Tell our listeners about your weapon, David.

D:

I went to the brook and picked out five smooth stones. I had my slingshot, and all it took was one — plop! — right in the forehead and down went Goliath.

R:

Pretty good shot, I'd say, and very courageous, David.

D:

Hey, it wasn't me alone — it was the Lord that won that battle.

R:

Thank you for your time, David. I think that we may see more of this young hero in the years ahead.

As the reporter interviews David, all the other characters are sitting around and watching. Essentially, it is a skit, with everyone taking turns participating, and with the tape recorder as the prop that pulls it together.

Obviously, this works best with older elementary children, most of whom seem to have a flair for the dramatic. Very young children will clam up entirely. Children in the primary grades may have fun with this, as long as they are allowed to do it their way and are free not to participate if they should so choose.

If the children know about this well ahead of time, they will "research their parts" by reading time-worn Bible stories with new eyes. This game forces them to "get inside" Bible characters and imagine what it was like for them. It also encourages them to learn and remember the details of the Biblical accounts as they relate to the history of God's saving His people.

Numerous other games can be similarly modified to incorporate Biblical themes. Pin the tail on the donkey can become "Pin the tail on Balaam's donkey." (Many will be surprised to know that the Bible tells of a time when a donkey actually talked. In fact, ask the children how many believe that there is such a story in the Bible. You can find the account in Numbers 22.) A bean bag toss can be called "Clobber Goliath," with a drawing of a large, ugly face for the target. Indoor or outdoor relay races can reflect the "relay race" between Elijah and Ahab (see 1 Kings 18:44-46). The possibilities are endless. Let your imagination, and the "personality" of your family, be your guide as you begin a new family tradition for celebrating the eve of All Saints' Day.

Being thus arrived in a good harbor, and brought safe to land, they fell upon their knees and blessed the God of Heaven who had brought them over the vast and furious ocean, and delivered them from all the perils and miseries thereof, again to set their feet on the firm and stable earth, their proper element.

William Bradford, 1590-1657
Of Plymouth Plantation

NINE

THE GOD WHO PROVIDES

Thanksgiving

In her powerful autobiography, *The Hiding Place*, Corrie Ten Boom recounts a poignant lesson in the discipline of thanksgiving. She and her sister Betsie were committed to a women's extermination camp under the Nazi regime. The huge dormitory to which they were assigned was packed to the gills, stinking, and worst of all, crawling with fleas. Desperately, they prayed that God would show them a way to endure these conditions.

In a flash, Betsie remembered the verse they had read that very morning from First Thessalonians: "Give thanks in all circumstances." They began to thank God aloud for all the various circumstances they now encountered. Corrie could not believe her ears, however, when Betsie sincerely thanked the Lord for the fleas. She was sure that Betsie was wrong in being grateful for the horrid, biting creatures.

Although the soldiers and guards cruelly mistreated the prisoners when the women were out and about, they never entered the dormitory room of the barracks. Unyielding guards patrolled all the barracks but theirs. Inside Barracks 28, however, Corrie and Betsie were free to conduct worship services, encouraging the other prisoners with Bible reading and prayer. The Ten Boom sisters were mystified by this freedom.

One day Betsie discovered the reason for their unwarranted freedom. The guards refused to go into Barracks 28 because of the fleas. Only then did they realize why they had every reason to be grateful to God—especially for the fleas.

For the Christian, Thanksgiving is not an annual holiday, it is a lifestyle. A spirit of thankfulness marks the person who truly loves Jesus Christ. Gratitude for His great sacrifice for us motivates our obedience, checks our sinfulness, and fans into flame our love and devotion to Him.

Yet we don't always feel thankful. Like Corrie Ten Boom, we wonder what in the world there is to be thankful about as we look at our circumstances. When hardship comes, the natural reaction is one of anger, resentment, and complaining. Thanksgiving seems absurd at such a time.

God's Word, however, does not command us to feel thankful, rather to give thanks. Thanksgiving is something one can do, whether one feels like it or not. It is a discipline, like prayer. Someone once said, "Pray when you feel like it, pray when you don't feel like it, and pray until you feel like it." The same can be said about thanksgiving. It is an act of the will, a recognition of God's goodness and provision in our lives. Thanksgiving is to take place in solitary prayer, in corporate worship, in casual conversation, and in our thought life as we go about our day. Emotions sometimes accompany thanksgiving. More often they follow the act of giving thanks. Many times the feelings simply are not there at all — the business of giving thanks is a mere act of obedience, nothing more, nothing less.

Surprisingly, it is not during hard times that it is most difficult to give thanks. Days of ease lure us from our dependency on God. We forget whose hand gave us all the good things we enjoy. A voice whispers to us that "we've earned it; we deserve it." Instead of being grateful for our prosperity, we find ourselves complaining about the things that irritate or inconvenience us.

Little do we realize what a great sin against God this is. Paul gives us a glimpse at the seriousness of thanklessness in the first chapter of his letter to the Romans. He writes about God's wrath against mankind when man turned his back on God: "For although they knew God, they neither glorified him as God nor gave thanks to him, but their thinking became futile and their foolish hearts were darkened" (Romans 1:21).

It is of the utmost importance, therefore, that we cultivate a spirit of thankfulness, in our own lives and in our families. We cannot expect our children to be naturally thankful any more than we can expect them to be naturally "good." Thankfulness must be taught like any other quality: by example, by instruction, and by correction, but it should be genuine and not a form of putting on piety for show, because God wants our honesty, too. Thankful spirits will arise out of a pattern of thankfulness set in the home.

INTRODUCTION

Background

Thanksgiving finds its true roots in the earliest pages of human history. Eve gave thanks to God when she gave birth to Cain. Later, the naming of Seth was a tribute of thanksgiving to the God who provides. Sacrifices were offered to God, not only in repentence for sin, but also in thanksgiving and worship of God. When Noah emerged from the ark, he immediately erected an altar and offered a sacrifice to God. Thanksgiving was surely one of the primary elements of this act of worship.

God Himself instituted three yearly thanksgiving festivals to be observed by the Israelites. These were a part of the law that God gave Moses on Mount Sinai (Exodus 23:14-17). The first was the Feast of Unleavened Bread, commemorating God's deliverance of Israel from bondage in Egypt. The second was the Feast of Harvest, a festival of joy upon reaping the first fruits of the crops. The third thanksgiving feast was the Feast of Ingathering. This celebrated the ingathering of the crops at the end of the harvest, as well as remembering God's provision during Israel's years of wandering in the desert. Three times each year, Israel was to celebrate God's goodness with a feast of thanksgiving.

A spirit of thanksgiving characterized the early church. As the Holy Spirit touched men's lives and they realized what Jesus had done for them, their hearts overflowed with gratitude. The theme of thankfulness to God through our Lord Jesus Christ permeates the Epistles. From Genesis to Revelation, the people of God were those who gave thanks and praise to Him.

The courageous Christians who journeyed to a new world on the tiny Mayflower also trusted the God of the Scriptures. The Pilgrims came seeking freedom to worship God. They left home, family, and security, risking their very lives for this freedom. After an arduous transatlantic voyage, they landed in early December 1620, ill prepared to face a winter in the New England wilderness. Despite relatively mild weather, half of the colonists died during those first few months. When spring finally arrived, the small group of survivors planted and began to build. The Indians befriended them and taught them how to catch fish and plant corn. By harvest, they were established and prepared to meet the onslaught of winter. God had protected them and provided for their needs. A feast of Thanksgiving was their response to God's goodness and providence.

The Pilgrims must have been thankful for many things — an abundant harvest, the friendship of the Indians, the fact that illness had not claimed all their lives. Yet the purpose of the feast was not to focus on the gifts but to exalt the Giver.

Contemporary society has lost this most fundamental element of Thanksgiving. School children learn about friendship with the Indians, good food and family, but God is not mentioned. An attitude of thankfulness is taught; however, no one asks the question, "Thankful to whom?" Whom should we thank for all the blessings in our lives?

Here Christians need to speak out, loud and clear. While the culture gropes around the fringes of Thanksgiving, only believers can articulate the central message of this holiday: Every good gift comes from God. He provides food, safety, health, family, and friends — in addition to all the spiritual blessings belonging to those who are in Christ. Our lives are ultimately in His hands, and we are dependent on Him.

This message must first be entrusted to our children. This chapter attempts to equip parents with the tools to teach children an attitude of thankfulness to God.

Overview

The month of November is devoted to developing an attitude of thanksgiving, preparing spiritually for the Thanksgiving feast. Four weekly family times examine and celebrate various aspects of God's providence. The life of Elijah provides the basis for these family times.

Elijah was a prophet during hard times for the nation of Israel. At this point, God was not bestowing blessings on His people; He was withholding them. Idolatry and evil practices permeated the nation, beginning at the top, with wicked King Ahab and his notorious queen, Jezebel. God's own people had turned their backs on the One who had redeemed them from slavery and brought them to the promised land. They ignored His prophets and adulterated His worship. Finally God turned off the spigots of heaven, knowing that hunger and thirst were effective tools for getting people's attention. No rain fell for three years in the land of Israel. It was during this time of drought that God provided miraculously for Elijah and those to whom he ministered.

The first week looks at how God supplied food and drink for Elijah and for the widow at Zarephath. The second family time examines God's provision of health and family as the widow's son experienced illness, death, then restoration to life. When Elijah is burned out, depressed, and lonely, God gives him a friend, Elisha. This is the subject of the third family time in November. At last, God bestows on Elijah the ultimate gift — eternal life. The fourth week, the family observes Elijah's amazing exit and explores how God provides eternal life for us today.

Specific Instructions

Several activities reinforce these lessons in thankfulness. A Thanksgiving banner utilizes the traditional horn of plenty to remind the family of God's gracious gifts. A simpler alternative is a real horn of plenty. As the horn fills up with fruit and vegetables (artificial or nonperishable), the family recognizes God's provision of food, family, friends, and eternal life.

During the month of November, the family keeps a basket in the middle of their table. Each family time, family members write down things for which they are thankful and put the slips of paper in the basket. By Thanksgiving Day, the basket is filled up with personalized "thank yous" to God.

Thanksgiving Day is an occasion of real family worship and thanksgiving to God. A family worship service is given, along with suggestions to make the before-dinner-prayer and the meal-time conversation focus on God and His good gifts.

FAMILY PROJECT

Two options are given for Thanksgiving family projects, both utilizing the idea of the Horn of Plenty. The first is a felt banner to decorate a wall. Felt pieces of fruit are added each week of November, illustrating the bountiful provision of God. The second, and simpler, option is a purchased wicker horn of plenty that can be filled up with fruit by the family.

Thanksgiving Banner (Option 1)

Materials

- 1 yard of 36-inch-wide green felt
- Green thread to match felt
- Tacky glue (glue for fabrics)
- 1 dowel, ⅜-inch diameter, 26 inches long
- Felt sheets (8½" × 11") in the following colors and quantities: yellow (1), light green (1), red (1), purple (1), orange (1), brown (1).
- 6 adhesive-back Velcro fasteners (black circles)
- 1 length of cord, ⅛-inch in diameter, 36 inches long
- 6 self-adhesive labels (1½" × 2¾")
- Black marking pen

Instructions

1. Cut the banner from the yard of green felt. The dimensions of the banner should be 22 inches by 36 inches (see Figure 9A). The leftover green felt will be used to make backings for the pieces of fruit.

2. Fold top edge (22 inch or narrow side) of banner over to the back side 1½ inches (see Figure 9B).

3. Sew overlap 1 inch from fold and ½ inch from edge, as shown in Figure 9B. This forms the casing for the dowel.

4. Trace and cut out the patterns on pp. 260-262.

5. Cut out the felt pieces for each of the patterns cut in Step 4. Colors and quantities are noted on the patterns.

6. Glue the horn of plenty on the banner as shown in Figure 9C. Use tacky glue to affix the horn to the banner.

7. Glue each piece of fruit to its corresponding green backing as shown in Figure 9D.

8. Apply adhesive side of hook (fuzzy) Velcro fasteners to the center of the back of each piece of fruit.

9. Arrange the fruit on the banner as shown in Figure 9E. Apply the loop Velcro fasteners to the green felt banner in the spots that correspond to the hook fasteners on the backs of the fruit pieces.

10. Drill a hole in the dowel ¾ inch from each end (see Figure 9F). If a drill is not available, use Option 2 in Step 11.

11. Insert dowel into casing.

12. *Option 1*
Stiffen ends of cord by wrapping with tape. Draw ends of cord through holes at ends of dowel and knot or tie cord (see Figure 9G).

Option 2
Tie cord around ends of dowel. Glue cord to dowel so that cord will not slide toward center when hung (see Figure 9H).

Using the Thanksgiving Banner

Remove the fruit from the banner. At the conclusion of each family time in November, one or two pieces of fruit will be added to the banner, filling out the horn of plenty by Thanksgiving.

Keep the felt pieces of fruit in a zip-lock bag alongside your Bible and *Family Celebrations*. Also place in the bag six self-adhesive labels and a black marking pen. Each piece of fruit will have a label that displays what the fruit represents (corn represents food, grapes represent family, pumpkin represents health, pear represents friends, and apples represent eternal life).

At the appropriate time, a parent will write down on the label what it is that God provided in the Bible story. A child will affix the label to the appropriate piece of fruit, then put the piece of fruit up on the banner. By Thanksgiving, the horn of plenty will be overflowing with fruit, reminding the family of all the good things that God gives us.

Horn of Plenty Basket with Real Fruit (Option 2)

For a simple alternative to the banner, buy a real horn of plenty (a wicker basket in the shape of a horn) and real fruits and vegetables. This can be used in the same way as the banner.

Materials
- One wicker basket in the shape of a horn of plenty (or regular basket)
- Autumn fruits and vegetables that will last through the month, such as:
- Indian corn
- Various squashes
- Small pumpkin
- Apples (red and golden)
- Pears

For perishable fruits, keep them in the refrigerator and take them out for the weekly family times during November. Imperishable fruits, such as Indian corn, may remain on display.

Using the Horn of Plenty

Each family time will focus on something that God provides. Select a different fruit or vegetable for each family time in November. At the appropriate time, have one of the children add the new fruit to the horn of plenty. This new fruit will represent that which God provided in the Bible story and which he also provides in our lives (food, family, health, friends, and eternal life).

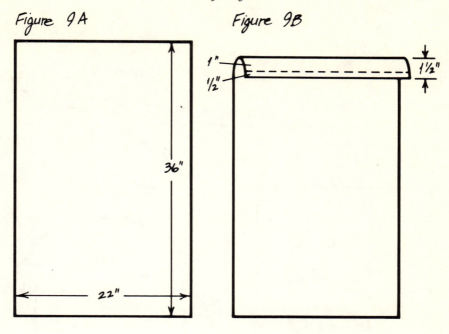

Figure 9A

36"

22"

Figure 9B

1"

1/2"

1½"

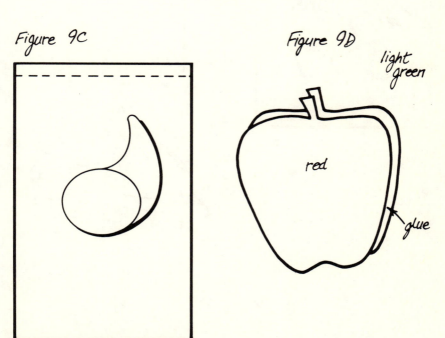

Figure 9C

Figure 9D

light green

red

glue

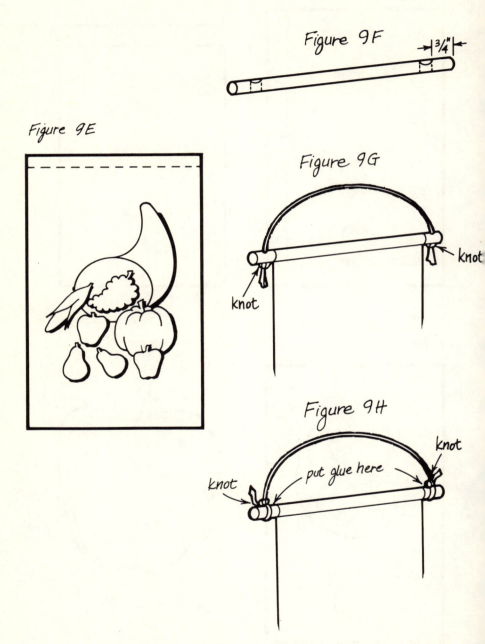

Figure 9F

3/4"

Figure 9E

Figure 9G

knot

knot

Figure 9H

knot

put glue here

knot

Another Alternative

You may also use plastic fruit with your real horn of plenty. Spoilage is then not a concern.

FAMILY TIMES AROUND GOD'S WORD

First Week in November — God Provides Food

Explain:

The Bible tells us that all good gifts come from God (James 1:17). Everything we have that is good is a gift from our loving heavenly Father. When we have all that we need, however, it is sometimes hard to remember this. We may start to think that we earned it and we deserve it, forgetting that God is the one who gave us good minds and strong bodies to work for a living. We forget that God sends the sun and the rain to grow crops, and without His goodness, the shelves of the grocery stores would be empty.

Back in the days of Elijah the prophet, the Israelites also forgot about God. They began to worship false gods and idols and do many things that made God unhappy. Finally God told them that He would not let it rain until they remembered Him. Soon the rivers and streams stopped running and the ground dried up. All the crops turned brown so that there was no grain for bread. Even the animals became skinnier and skinnier, and they too started to die.

Read:
1 Kings 17:1-16

Discuss:

1. Ahab was the wicked king of Israel. What was the bad news that Elijah brought him? Why do you think Elijah had to go away to hide?

2. How did God provide for Elijah when he was hiding from King Ahab? Why did God take special care of Elijah?

3. When the brook dried up, what did God tell Elijah to do?

4. A widow is a woman whose husband has died. Because she had no husband, she was probably poor. What did she say when Elijah asked her for a piece of bread? What did Elijah tell her to do?

5. How did God provide food for the woman and her son? How do you think she felt about this?

6. How does God provide food for you and your family? This week as you pray before meals, remember to thank Him, not only for the food, but for all He gives us so that we can have food. (Examples: rain, sun, seasons, our bodies and minds, health, energy)

Memorize:

Psalm 23:1

"The Lord is my shepherd; I shall lack nothing."

Pray:

Heavenly Father, thank You for providing for us. You give us everything we need to live—strong, healthy bodies and minds, sun and rain for the plants to grow. Forgive us for forgetting that all these things are gifts from Your hands, Lord. Give us thankful hearts, in Jesus' name. Amen.

Sing:

"All People that on Earth Do Dwell" (Old Hundredth, *HWC* 20)

> All people that on earth do dwell,
> Sing to the Lord with cheerful voice;
> Him serve with mirth, His praise forth tell,
> Come ye before Him, and rejoice.
>
> Know that the Lord is God indeed;
> Without our aid He did us make;
> We are His folk, He doth us feed,
> And for His sheep He doth us take.

Do:

Pass out slips of paper and pencils to all in the family who can write. Have everyone think of one thing for which he is thankful, especially relating to the basic necessities of life. Those who can write should do so. Mom or Dad can write for pre-schoolers. Fold up the slips of paper and place them in a basket in the center of the table. These special "thank you items" will be a part of the Thanksgiving celebration.

Second Week of November—God Provides Family

Explain:

Nothing makes us appreciate food like a hungry, growling stomach. The same thing is true of so many things in life. We don't really appreciate them until one day they aren't there.

This is especially true of our families. Have you ever gotten lost or separated from your mom or dad in a store? What did that feel like? Can you remember how happy you were to see their faces when they found you?

Today's story is about the same widow we read about last week. She and her son were about to die because they were almost out of food, but God gave them all they needed. In today's story, we find that the widow has lost the most important thing in the whole world to her—her son.

Read:
1 Kings 17:17-24

Discuss:

1. What happened to the boy? How did his mother feel?
2. What did Elijah do? What did God do?
3. What did the mother say when she saw her son alive again?
4. Did you know that God has given you each member of your family? And every day that you have together is a special gift from Him. When do you appreciate your family the most?
5. Go around in a circle, telling what you appreciate most about the person on your right. If you want, reverse directions and do the same for the person on your left.

Memorize:
Philippians 1:3

"I thank my God every time I remember you."

Pray:

Starting with the oldest member of the family, have each person say a brief thank-you prayer for the next member in order of age. For instance, Dad thanks God for Mom, Mom thanks God for the ten-year-old, the ten-year-old says thank you for the seven-year-old, who in turn thanks God for the five-year-old. The five-year-old completes the circle by thanking God for Dad.

Sing:

"For the Beauty of the Earth" (*HWC* 560)

> For the beauty of the earth,
> For the glory of the skies,
> For the love which from our birth
> Over and around us lies;
> Lord of all, to Thee we raise
> This our hymn of grateful praise.

> For the joy of human love,
> Brother, sister, parent, child;
> Friends on earth and friends above;
> For all gentle thoughts and mild:
> Lord of all, to Thee we raise
> This our hymn of grateful praise.

Third Week in November — God Provides Friends

Explain:

After three years of no rain, the people were desperate. Finally they were willing to listen to Elijah. Elijah suggested a test on the top of Mount Carmel. The priests of the false god, Baal, prayed for their god to send fire from heaven onto the altar they had built for him. All morning and afternoon, the 450 priests danced, sang, cried, and prayed, but of course nothing happened.

Then it was Elijah's turn. He tried to make his prayer seem even more impossible by having twelve jars of water poured on the offering and wood. Yet all he had to do was ask, and God sent fire from heaven. The fire consumed the sacrifice, the wood, the stones, the dirt, and even the water. The people were amazed and realized that Elijah's God was the only true God.

After the horrible priests of Baal were killed, and all the people had left, Elijah began to pray for rain. He prayed long and hard, and finally a tiny cloud was spotted. Before long, the sky was black with billowy storm clouds. Think of how thankful the people must have been as the heavy rains pounded the dry, cracked earth.

One person was not happy, however. The evil queen Jezebel hated God and was boiling with rage that Elijah's God had won over her priests of Baal. She sent a message to Elijah that she would have him killed within one day.

Read:
1 Kings 19

Discuss:
1. What did Elijah do when he heard that Jezebel was going to kill him? How was he feeling as he sat under the broom tree in the desert?

2. The Lord knew that he was tired and hungry and first needed sleep and food. After giving him the things his body needed, he sent Elijah to a mountain. What happened at the mountain? How did God speak to Elijah?

3. What was Elijah really upset about (see v. 14)? Elijah felt all alone. What do you think Elijah needed?

4. Did God give Elijah what he needed? Who was the friend that God gave to Elijah? Once Elijah had a partner and friend, Jezebel's threats didn't terrify him anymore.

5. Do you ever feel all alone? What do you think God wants you to do when you are feeling this way? Do you think that God can give you a friend like he did Elijah?

6. Think about the friends that God has given you. Go around the circle and tell the name of a special friend that God has given you.

Memorize:
James 1:17a

"Every good and perfect gift is from above."

Pray:

Dear Father, thank You for all the wonderful friends You have given us. They encourage us and help us and show us Your love. We appreciate those friendships so much and know that they too are good and perfect gifts from You. In Jesus' name we pray. Amen.

Sing:

"Praise to the Lord, the Almighty" (*HWC* 8)

> Praise to the Lord, the Almighty,
>   the King of Creation;
> O my soul, praise him, for he is thy health
>   and salvation:
> All ye who hear, now to his temple draw near;
> Joining in glad adoration.
>
> Praise to the Lord, who o'er all things
>   so wondrously reigneth,
> Shelters thee under His wings, yes,
>   so gently sustaineth:
> Hast thou not seen?
> How all thy longings have been
> Granted in what He ordaineth.

Do:

Pass out the slips of paper and pencils again to all in the family who can write. Have everyone think of one friend for whom he is especially thankful. Those who can write should do so. Mom or Dad can write for preschoolers. Fold up the slips of paper and place them in a basket in the center of the table. These special "thank-you items" will be a part of the Thanksgiving celebration.

Fourth Week of November — God Provides Eternal Life

Explain:

All his life, Elijah saw God provide in amazing ways. God provided food and bread for him during the dry years. God gave new life to the widow's son, restoring her family. Finally, God provided fire from heaven, rain after three years of drought, and a special helper for Elijah. Do you remember what that special friend's name was? It was Elisha. God was preparing Elisha to take Elijah's place, for the end of Elijah's life was near.

Read:
2 Kings 2:1-18

Discuss:
1. Why didn't Elisha want to leave Elijah?
2. What happened to Elijah?
3. How did Elisha know that he would have God's power now that Elijah was gone?
4. Where is Elijah now? How do you know?
5. Eternal life means life with God, starting now and ending never. Yes, it means going to heaven, but it also means having God's love and power in our lives right now, here on earth utterly as a gift. Read John 3:16 to find out how you can have eternal life. (You might want to ask your children, if you think it is appropriate, if they feel they have this life or not.)

Memorize:
John 3:16

"For God so loved the world that he gave his one and only Son, that whoever believes in him shall not perish but have eternal life."

Pray:
Dear Father, we thank You so much that You loved us enough to send Your Son to die for us. He is the greatest gift of all. Thank You for all that You give us because of Jesus. In Jesus' name. Amen.

Sing:
"Come, Thou Fount of Every Blessing" (*HWC* 2)

Come, thou Fount of every blessing,
Tune my heart to sing Thy grace;
Streams of mercy, never ceasing,
Call for songs of loudest praise.

Teach me some melodious sonnet
Sung by flaming tongues above;
Praise His name—I'm fixed upon it—
Name of God's redeeming love.

Hitherto Thy love has blest me;
Thou hast bro't me to this place;
And I know Thy hand will bring me
Safely home by Thy good grace.
Jesus sought me when a stranger,
Wand'ring from the fold of God;
He, to rescue me from danger,
Bought me with His precious blood.

O to grace how great a debtor
Daily I'm constrained to be!
Let Thy goodness, like a fetter,
Bind my wandering heart to Thee.
Prone to wander, Lord, I feel it,
Prone to leave the God I love;
Here's my heart, O take and seal it,
Seal it for Thy courts above.

Do:

Pass out the slips of paper and pencils again to all in the family who can write. Have everyone think of one thing God gives us when He gives us eternal life (e.g., love, peace, a home in heaven). Those who can write should do so. Mom or Dad can write for preschoolers. Fold up the slips of paper and place them in a basket in the center of the table. These special "thank-you items" will be a part of the Thanksgiving celebration.

FAMILY CELEBRATION

American tradition dictates that the turkey be the centerpiece of the Thanksgiving celebration. The delicious festive meal, shared with family and friends, deserves a place of prominence on this beloved holiday.

The food itself, however, should not eclipse the God who provided it. This can easily happen. Preparation for Thanksgiving dinner, and clean-up afterward, are quite a production. It is difficult to have your mind on spiritual things, and at the same time keep track of when the turkey comes out of the oven and how to keep your gravy from having lumps in it. For that reason, someone other than the "cook" must be responsible for the spiritual dimension of Thanksgiving.

Yet especially for Christian families, the focus of this celebration should be on the God who provides. Gratitude to God is a hallmark of the Christian life, and this day should be a climactic celebration of an entire year filled with thanksgiving.

Here are several suggestions for making your Thanksgiving a spiritual event in which the family focuses with thankful hearts on God's great goodness. First, ideas for the prayer and the mealtime conversation are given. Then there is an after-dinner time of family worship.

The Thanksgiving Meal

The Prayer

Before the meal, have one of the children pass out pencils and small slips of paper, three slips of paper for each person present. Instruct everyone to think of three things for which he is especially thankful. These things should be as specific (and brief) as possible. Write these three things on the three slips of paper. (Preschoolers may draw a picture of the things for which they are thankful.) Everyone should bring the slips of paper to the table when dinner is served.

The leader has a basket at his place. This may be the same basket that the family used during the pre-Thanksgiving family times. If so, it already has a number of slips of paper in it.

Starting with the person to the right of the leader, go around the table, each person offering thanks to God for the three things that they have written on their slips of paper. Pass the basket at the same time, so that the basket is always in front of the person who is giving thanks. After that person has finished giving thanks, she places her slips of paper in the basket and passes the basket on to the next person. Continue around the circle, until the basket is once again in front of the leader.

After the leader has given thanks for his three specific things, and placed his three slips of paper in the basket, he lifts the basket up and offers a prayer of general thanksgiving.

This is like taking an offering in church, except that this is an offering of thanks. God desires our thanks every bit as much as our money. The writer to the Hebrews instructs us, "Through Jesus, therefore, let us continually offer to God a sacrifice of praise — the fruit of lips that confess his name" (Hebrews 13:15).

The Meal

During the meal, let your conversation dwell on God's goodness to your family in the past year. Encourage each person to share one way in which God has helped him or her during the past twelve months. This will provide the basis for your "Litany of Thanksgiving," a family psalm that you will write after the meal, then recite together during family worship.

Litany of Thanksgiving

Write a family psalm of thanksgiving based on God's faithfulness and provision in the past. This psalm can be written during dinner (or discussed during dinner and written down afterward). Think together as a family about your past, and how God has provided for you in specific situations. Write down how God helped you in each of these circumstances, using short psalm-like sentences. As a model, see Psalm 136 (on pp. 155-159 of this book). Recite your family psalm during your family worship celebration on Thanksgiving. Each person takes a turn, and the rest of the family joins in the refrain: "Your love endures forever."

You may want to have one of the children copy your family psalm neatly on a sheet of white paper and glue it to colorful construction paper or posterboard. Then post it somewhere as a constant reminder to your family to be thankful for God's work in your lives.

Family Worship on Thanksgiving Day

Call to Worship

Leader:
Praise the Lord.
Give thanks to the Lord, for He is good;

All:
His love endures forever.

Leader:
1 Chronicles 29:10-13:

"Praise be to you, O Lord,
    God of our father Israel,
    from everlasting to everlasting.
Yours, O Lord, is the greatness and the power
    and the glory and the majesty and the splendor,
    for everything in heaven and earth is yours.
Yours, O Lord, is the kingdom;
    you are exalted as head over all.
Wealth and honor come from you;
    you are the ruler of all things.
In your hands are strength and power
    to exalt and give strength to all.
Now, our God, we give you thanks,
    and praise your glorious name."

Sing:
"Come, Ye Thankful People, Come" (*HWC* 559)

Come, ye thankful people come—
Raise the song of harvest-home:
All is safely gathered in
Ere the winter storms begin.
God, our Maker, doth provide
For our wants to be supplied:
Come to God's own temple, come—
Raise the song of harvest-home.

Litany of Thanksgiving
Recite the litany of Thanksgiving as described above.

Sing:
"Now Thank We All Our God" (*HWC* 556)

Now thank we all our God
With heart and hands and voices,
Who wondrous things hath done,
In whom His world rejoices;
Who, from our mother's arms,
Hath blessed us on our way

With countless gifts of love,
And still is ours today.

O may this bounteous God
Through all our life be near us,
With ever joyful hearts
And blessed peace to cheer us;
And keep us in His grace,
And guide us when perplexed,
And free us from all ills
In this world and the next.

All praise and thanks to God
The Father now be given,
The Son, and Him who reigns
With them in highest heaven:
The one eternal God,
Whom earth and heaven adore;
For thus it was, is now,
And shall be evermore. Amen.

Dismissal:

Leader:

Praise be to the Lord, the God of Israel, from everlasting to everlasting. Let all the people say,

All:

Amen! Praise the Lord!

HYMN INDEX

Here follows an alphabetical listing of the hymns used in this book. The texts for all these hymns are in the public domain and are reprinted as found in *The Hymnal for Worship and Celebration*, Word Music, Waco, TX, 1986. Also given are the hymn numbers as designated in the aforementioned hymnal (*HWC*) and the page numbers where portions of the text are given in this book.

"Christ the Lord is Risen Today" (*HWC* 217) p. 94 (Charles Wesley, Lyra Davidica)

"Come, Thou Fount of Every Blessing" (*HWC* 2) p. 223 (Robert Robinson, trad. American melody)

"Come, Thou Long-Expected Jesus" (*HWC* 124) p. 23 (Charles Wesley, Rowland H. Prichard)

"Come, Ye Sinners, Poor and Needy" (*HWC* 334) p. 76 (Joseph Hart, trad. American Melody)

"Come, Ye Thankful People, Come" (*HWC* 559) p. 227 (Henry Alford, George J. Elvey)

"Crown Him With Many Crowns" (*HWC* 234) pp. 84, 95 (Matthew Bridges, George J. Elvey)

"Faith of Our Fathers" (*HWC* 279) p. 196 (Frederick W. Faber, Henry F. Henry)

"For the Beauty of the Earth" (*HWC* 560) p. 220 (Folliott S. Pierpoint, Conrad Kocher)

"God of Our Fathers" (*HWC* 573) pp. 126, 142, 143 (Daniel C. Roberts, Geo. W. Warren)

"Good Christian Men, Rejoice" (*HWC* 151) pp. 24, 38 (Latin carol, German melody)

"Guide Me, O Thou Great Jehovah" (*HWC* 51) pp. 141, 153 (Wm. Williams, John Hughes)

"Hallelujah, What a Savior!" (*HWC* 175) pp. 77, 79 (Philip P. Bliss)

"Hark! the Herald Angels Sing" (*HWC* 133) pp. 25, 28, 46 (Charles Wesley, Felix Mendelssohn)

"How Firm a Foundation" (*HWC* 275) p. 194 (Rippon's *Selection of Hymns*, 1787, trad. American melody)

"I Lay My Sins on Jesus" (*HWC* 340) p. 85 (Horatius Bonar, trad. Greek melody)

"Immortal, Invisible" (*HWC* 25) p. 159 (Walter Chalmers Smith, Welsh melody)

"Jesus Paid It All" (*HWC* 210) p. 86 (Elvina M. Hall, John T. Grape)

"Jesus, Priceless Treasure" (*HWC* 413) p. 56 (Johann Franck, trad. German melody)

"The Church's One Foundation" (*HWC* 277) p. 192 (Samuel J. Stone, Samuel S. Wesley)

"The King of Love My Shepherd Is" (*HWC* 468) pp. 58, 75 (Henry W. Baker, John B. Dykes)

"Thou Didst Leave Thy Throne" (*HWC* 127) p. 26 (Emily E. S. Elliott, Timothy R. Matthews)

"Were You There?" (*HWC* 181) p. 92 (traditional spiritual)

"What A Friend We Have in Jesus" (*HWC* 435) pp. 128, 146 (Joseph M. Scriven, Charles C. Converse)

"What Child Is This?" (*HWC* 137) pp. 32, 39 (William C. Dix, Trad. English melody)

"When I Survey the Wondrous Cross" (*HWC* 185) pp. 81, 83 (Isaac Watts; Gregorian chant, arr. by Lowell Mason)

"Who Is On the Lord's Side?" (*HWC* 484) p. 150 (Francis Ridley Havergal, C. Luis Reichardt)

SYMBOL PATTERNS

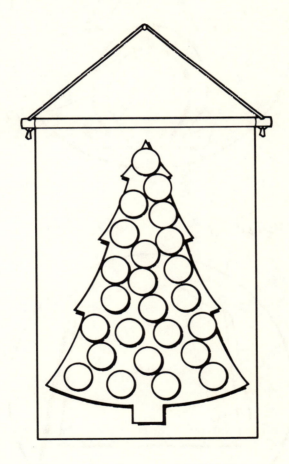

Christmas Tree Banner

Symbol 1A

purple

white

purple

Symbol 1B

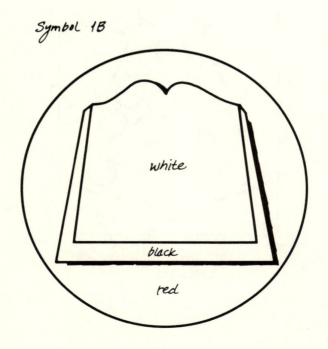

white

black

red

Symbol 1C

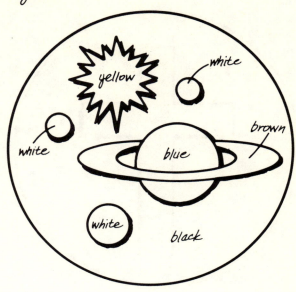

Symbol 1D

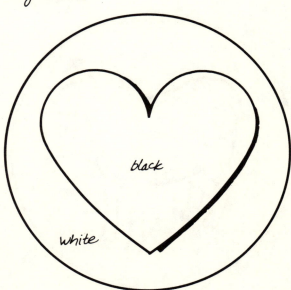

Symbol 1E

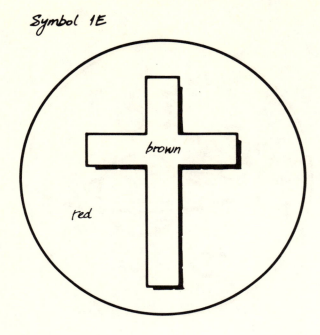

brown

red

Symbol 1F

white

red

Symbol 1G

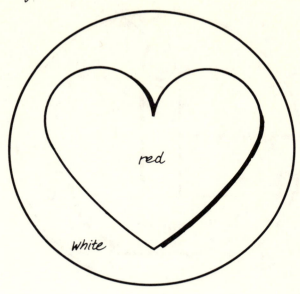

red

white

Symbol 1H

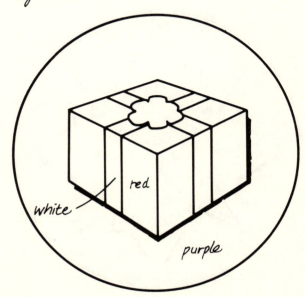

red

white

purple

Symbol 1I

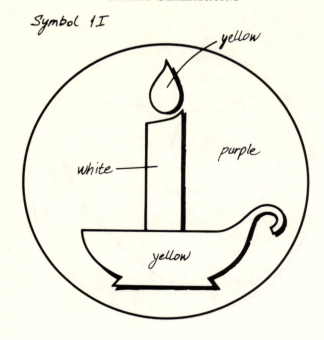

Symbol 1J

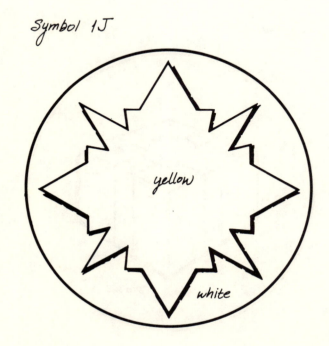

Symbol 1K

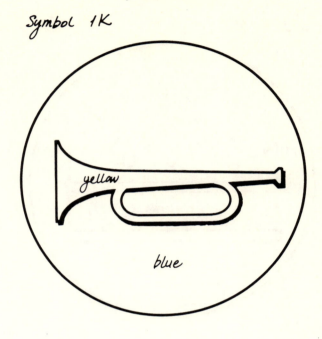

yellow

blue

Symbol 1L

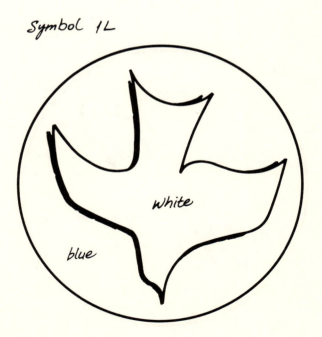

white

blue

Symbol 1M

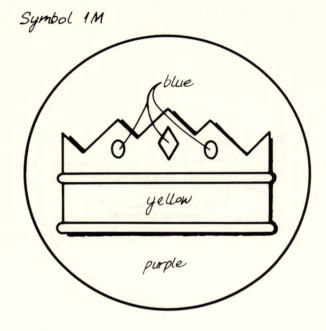

blue

yellow

purple

Symbol 1N

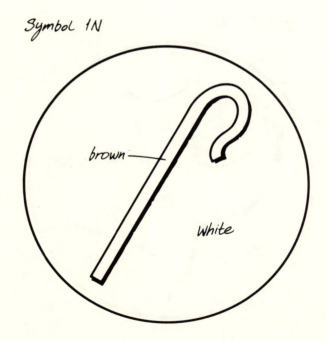

brown

White

Symbol 10

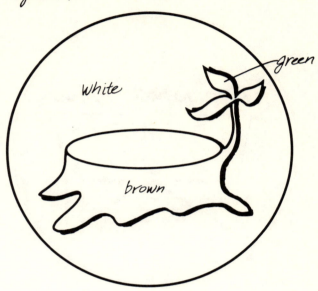

Symbol 1P

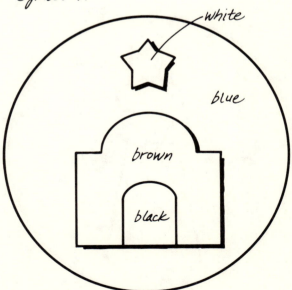

Symbol 1Q

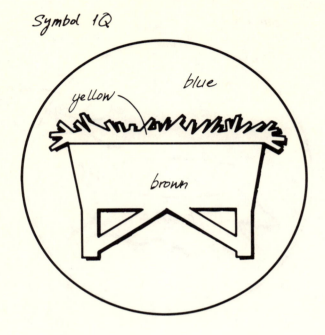

Symbol 1R

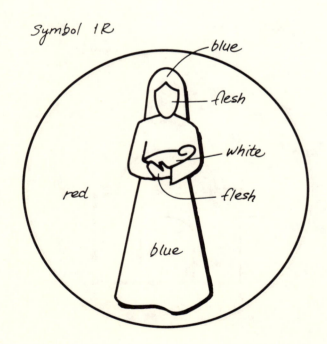

Symbol 1S

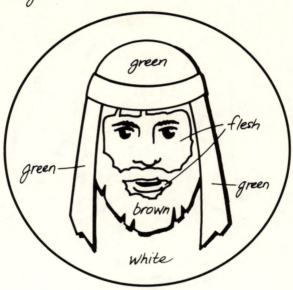

green

flesh

green

green

brown

white

Symbol 1T

yellow

flesh

white

purple

Symbol 1U

blue

white

Symbol 1V

red

black

black

Symbol 1W

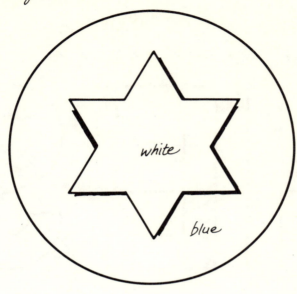

white

blue

Symbol 1X

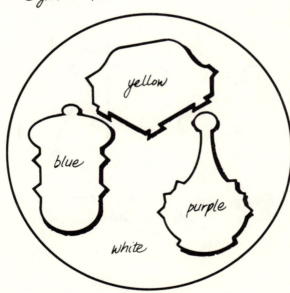

yellow

blue

purple

white

Cut these letters out of purple felt.

Enlarge these letters to 150 %
on a Copy Machine before tracing.

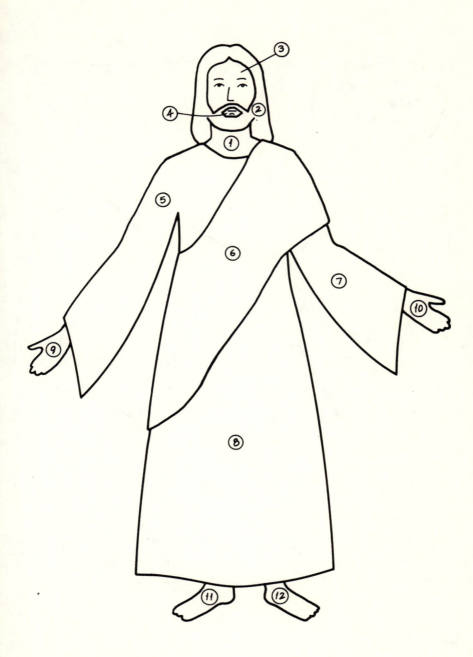

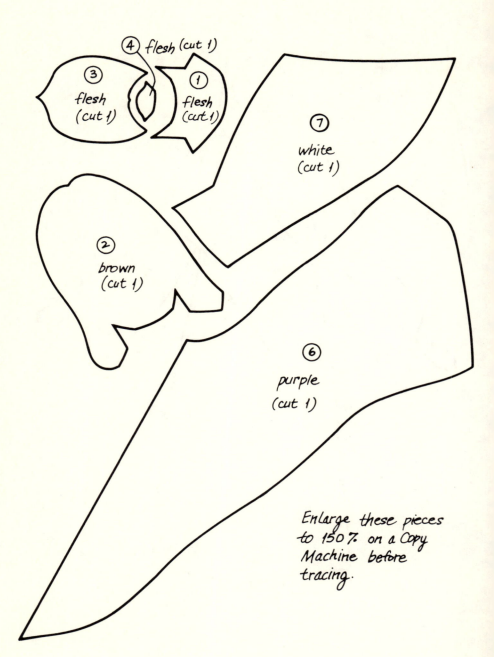

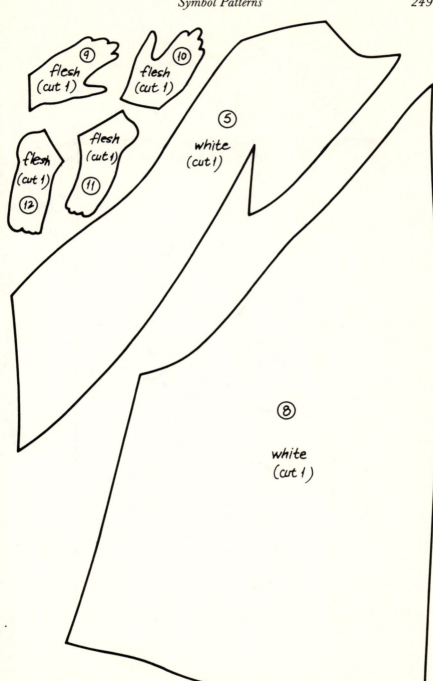

flesh
(cut 1) ⑨

flesh
(cut 1) ⑩

flesh
(cut 1) ⑪

flesh
(cut 1) ⑫

⑤ white
(cut 1)

⑧

white
(cut 1)

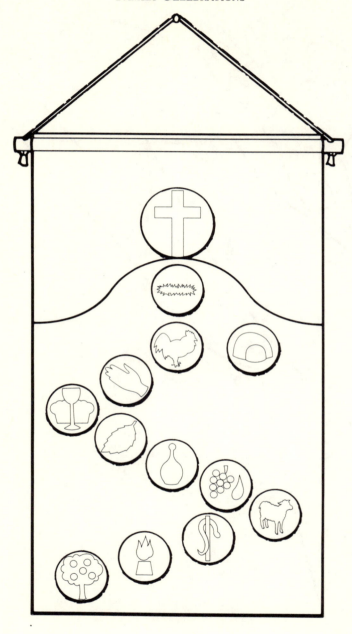

Road to Calvary Banner

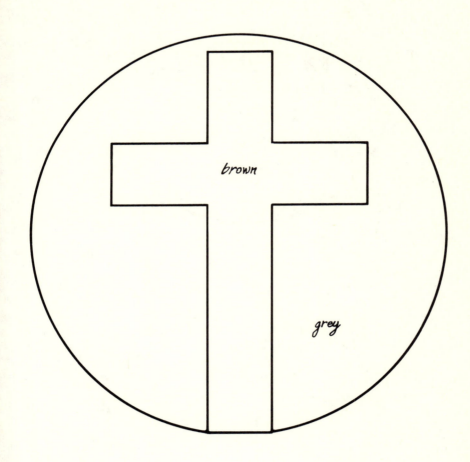

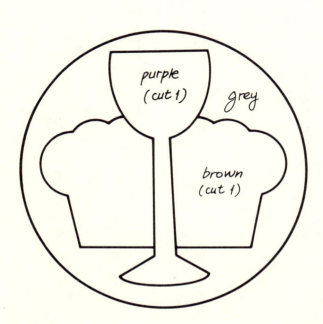

white
(cut 1)

grey

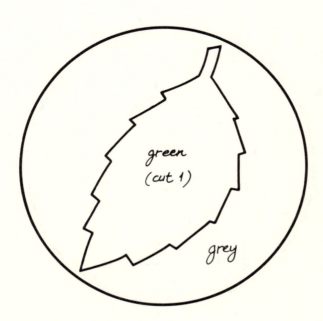

green
(cut 1)

grey

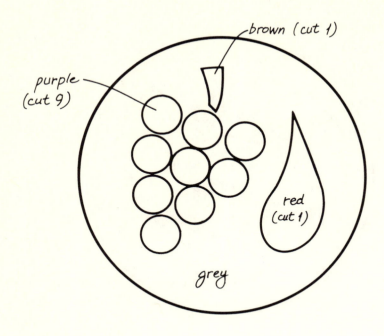

brown (cut 1)

purple (cut 9)

red (cut 1)

grey

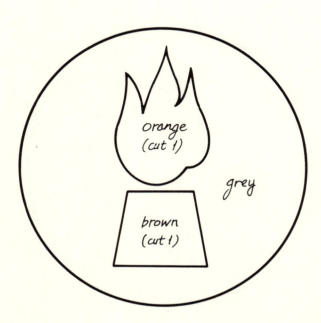

orange (cut 1)

grey

brown (cut 1)

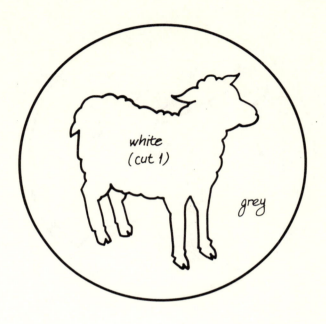

white
(cut 1)

grey

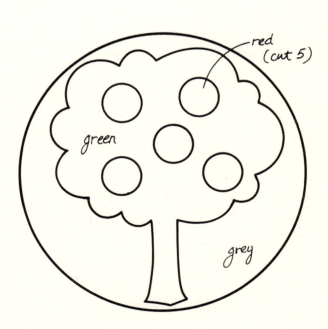

red
(cut 5)

green

grey

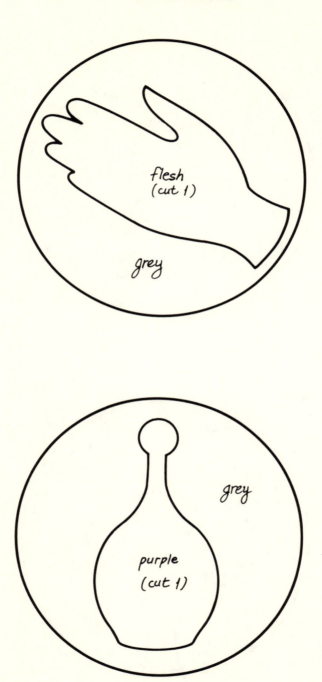

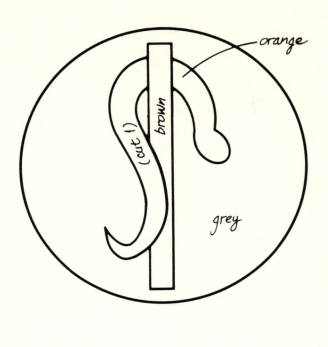

orange

(cut 1)

brown

grey

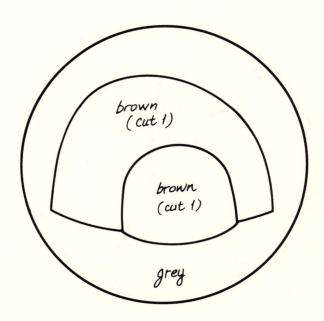

brown
(cut 1)

brown
(cut 1)

grey

Symbol 4A

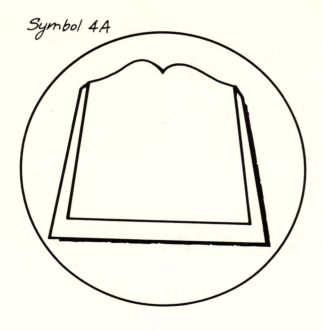

Symbol 4B

Symbol 4C

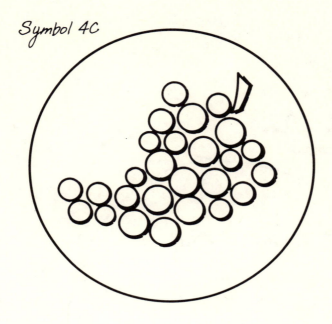

Symbol 4D

Thanksgiving Banner
Symbol 9A

★ Enlarge each to 300% on a Copy Machine before tracing.

Horn of Plenty

(1) Brown

Symbol 9B

★ Make one Dark Green backing for each of the fruits.

Pumpkin

(1) Orange

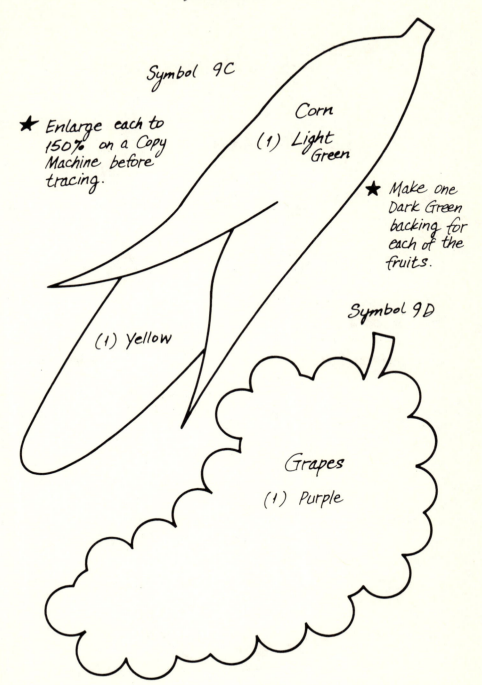

Symbol 9C

★ Enlarge each to 150% on a Copy Machine before tracing.

Corn
(1) Light Green

★ Make one Dark Green backing for each of the fruits.

(1) Yellow

Symbol 9D

Grapes
(1) Purple

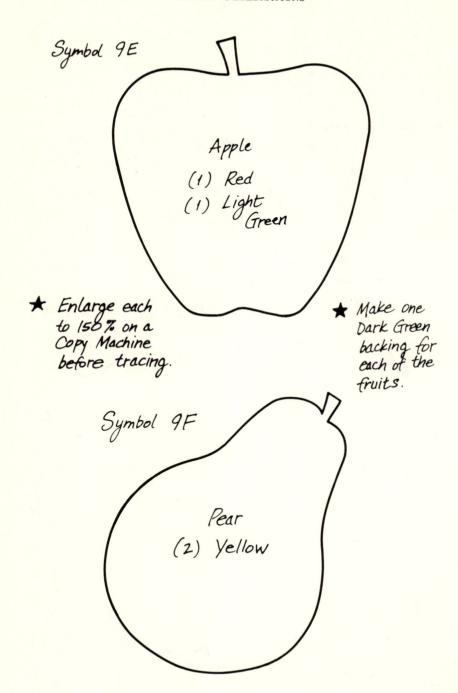

Symbol 9E

Apple

(1) Red

(1) Light Green

★ Enlarge each to 150% on a Copy Machine before tracing.

★ Make one Dark Green backing for each of the fruits.

Symbol 9F

Pear

(2) Yellow

MISSION STATEMENT
for Wolgemuth & Hyatt, Publishers, Inc.

The mission of Wolgemuth & Hyatt, Publishers, Inc., is to publish and distribute books that lead individuals toward:

- A personal faith in the one true God: Father, Son, and Holy Spirit;
- A lifestyle of practical discipleship; and
- A worldview that is consistent with the historic, Christian faith.

Moreover, the company will endeavor to accomplish this mission at a reasonable profit and in a manner which glorifies God and serves His Kingdom.

COLOPHON

The typeface for the text of this book is *Baskerville*. Its creator, John Baskerville (1706-1775), broke with tradition to reflect in his type the rounder, yet more sharply cut lettering of eighteenth-century stone inscriptions and copy books. The type foreshadows modern design in such novel characteristics as the increase in contrast between thick and thin strokes and the shifting of stress from the diagonal to the vertical strokes. Realizing that this new style of letter would be most effective if cleanly printed on smooth paper with genuinely black ink, he built his own presses, developed a method of hot-pressing the printed sheet to a smooth, glossy finish, and experimented with special inks. However, Baskerville did not enter into general commercial use in England until 1923.

Substantive editing by George Grant
Copy editing by Stephen Hines
Cover design by Kent Puckett Associates, Atlanta, Georgia
Typography by Thoburn Press, Tyler, Texas
Printed and bound by Maple-Vail Book Manufacturing Group
Manchester, Pennsylvania
Cover Printing by Weber Graphics, Chicago, Illinois